# Campaign Finance Reform

# LEXINGTON STUDIES IN POLITICAL COMMUNICATION

**Series Editor: Robert E. Denton, Jr.,**
**Virginia Polytechnic Institute and State University**

This series encourages focused work examining the role and function of communication in the realm of politics including campaigns and elections, media, and political institutions.

## TITLES IN SERIES:

*Governing Codes: Gender, Metaphor, and Political Identity*, By Karrin Vasby Anderson and Kristina Horn Sheeler
*Paving the Way for Madam President*, By Nichola D. Gutgold
*Maryland Politics and Political Communication, 1950–2005*, By Theodore F. Sheckels
*Images, Issues, and Attacks: Television Advertising by Incumbents and Challengers in Presidential Elections*, By E. D. Dover
*Democracy as Discussion: Civic Education and the American Forum Movement*, By William Keith
*Picturing China in the American Press: The Visual Portrayal of Sino-American Relations in* Time *Magazine, 1949–1973*, By David D. Perlmutter
*Lottery Wars: Case Studies in Bible Belt Politics, 1986–2005*, By Randy Bobbitt
*Post-9/11 American Presidential Rhetoric: A Study of Protofascist Discourse*, By Colleen Elizabeth Kelley
*Making a Difference: A Comparative View of the Role of the Internet in Election Politics*, Edited by Stephen Ward, Diana Owen, Richard Davis, and David Taras
*Seen and Heard: The Women of Television News*, By Nichola D. Gutgold
*Nuclear Legacies: Communication, Controversy, and the U. S. Nuclear Weapons Complex*, Edited by Bryan C. Taylor, William J. Kinsella, Stephen P. Depoe, Maribeth S. Metzler
*Conditional Press Influence in Politics*, By Adam J. Schiffer
*Telling Political Lives: The Rhetorical Autobiographies of Women Leaders in the United States*, Edited by Brenda DeVore Marshall and Molly A. Mayhead
*Media Bias? A Comparative Study of Time, Newsweek, the National Review, and the Progressive, 1975–2000*, By Tawnya J. Adkins Covert and Philo C. Wasburn
*Navigating the Post–Cold War World: President Clinton's Foreign Policy Rhetoric*, By Jason A. Edwards
*The Rhetoric of Pope John Paul II*, Edited by Joseph R. Blaney and Joseph P. Zompetti
*Stagecraft and Statecraft: Advance and Media Events in Political Communication*, By Dan Schill
*Rhetorical Criticism: Perspectives in Action*, Edited by Jim A. Kuypers
*Almost Madam President: Why Hillary Clinton "Won" in 2008*, By Nichola D. Gutgold
*Cracked But Not Shattered: Hillary Rodham Clinton's Unsuccessful Run for the Presidency*, Edited by Theodore F. Sheckels
*Gender and Political Communication in America: Rhetoric, Representation, and Display*, Edited by Janis L. Edwards
*Communicator-in-Chief: How Barack Obama Used New Media Technology to Win the White House*, Edited by John Allen Hendricks and Robert E. Denton, Jr.
*Centrist Rhetoric: The Production of Political Transcendence in the Clinton Presidency*, By Antonio de Velasco
*Studies of Identity in the 2008 Presidential Campaign*, Edited by Robert E. Denton, Jr.
*Campaign Finance Reform: The Political Shell Game*, By Melissa M. Smith, Glenda C. Williams, Larry Powell, and Gary A. Copeland
*Us against Them: The Political Culture of Talk Radio*, By Randy Bobbitt

# Campaign Finance Reform

## The Political Shell Game

Melissa M. Smith, Glenda C. Williams,
Larry Powell, and Gary A. Copeland

LEXINGTON BOOKS
A division of
ROWMAN & LITTLEFIELD PUBLISHERS, INC.
*Lanham • Boulder • New York • Toronto • Plymouth, UK*

Published by Lexington Books
A division of Rowman & Littlefield Publishers, Inc.
A wholly owned subsidiary of The Rowman & Littlefield Publishing Group, Inc.
4501 Forbes Boulevard, Suite 200, Lanham, Maryland 20706
http://www.lexingtonbooks.com

Estover Road, Plymouth PL6 7PY, United Kingdom



British Library Cataloguing in Publication Information Available

**Library of Congress Cataloging-in-Publication Data**

Campaign finance reform : the political shell game / Melissa M. Smith ... [et al.].
p. cm. — (Lexington studies in political communication)
Includes bibliographical references and index.
ISBN 978-0-7391-4565-4 (cloth : alk. paper) — ISBN 978-0-7391-4566-1 (pbk. : alk. paper) — ISBN 978-0-7391-4567-8 (electronic)
1. Campaign funds—United States. 2. Campaign funds—Law and legislation—United States. I. Smith, Melissa M., 1963-
JK1991.C3445 2010
324.7'80973—dc22 2010006992

∞™ The paper used in this publication meets the minimum requirements of American National Standard for Information Sciences—Permanence of Paper for Printed Library Materials, ANSI/NISO Z39.48-1992.

Printed in the United States of America

# Contents

**Future of Campaign Finance Reform**

# 1

# Overview of Campaign Finance Law

*Glenda C. Williams*

## EARLY HISTORY

The campaign finance reform debate began more than 100 years ago, long before even the invention of radio or television.[1] During the elections of 1896 and 1900, corporations, banks, railroads, and other businesses had poured enormous amounts of money into political coffers. William McKinley raised millions of dollars in his bid for the presidency, leading to questions of whether companies were buying his influence.[2] However, it was not until after the election scandals of 1904 involving President Theodore Roosevelt (who was accused by his opponent, Judge Alton Parker, of being "bought") that reformers were successful in bringing about change in campaign finance laws.[3] This took the shape of the Tillman Act, named for its author, Rep. Benjamin Tillman, and passed by congress in 1907.[4] The Tillman Act banned contributions from banks and corporations for all candidates for federal office.

Other acts soon followed. The Federal Corrupt Practices Act (a.k.a. the Publicity Act of 1910) required disclosure of money received and spent by any party or committee running elections in more than one state.[5] As these disclosures were made after the election, the overall effect on campaign finance practice was minimal. In 1911, congress amended the Publicity Act requiring all federal candidates to disclose contributions both before and after the election, whether the primary or general election.[6] Campaign spending limits were also invoked by the amendments, but were struck down by the Supreme Court in 1921.[7]

A new scandal paved the way for more reform in 1924 when federal office-holders accepted "donations" in an off year. These contributions were given to those in decision-making positions on prominent committees in charge of determining who would be granted oil leases. The contributors were oil development companies.[8] This led to the Federal Corrupt Practices Act of 1925, which brought all campaign finance legislation under one comprehensive code.[9] The Act required quarterly disclosure reports for each year served. The spending limits were revised to allow $25,000 for Senate races and $5,000 for House races.[10] In practice, however, the Act did very little to reform campaign financing. Information (and thus disclosures) was not easily provided to the public, and the act's wording provided large loopholes allowing many to continue raising and spending money as before.[11]

The Hatch Act of 1939 (a.k.a. the Clean Politics Act) sponsored by Sen. Carl Hatch (D-NM) restricted non-elected federal employees (such as civil servants and bureaucrats) from political activity; most specifically, it restricted them from soliciting contributions for campaigns.[12] The Hatch Act was amended in 1940 to limit individual contributions to federal candidates or national committees to $5,000 per individual.[13] However, state and local parties were not included in the restrictions, and therefore the Act did little to decrease campaign war chests.[14]

Roosevelt's policies regarding the New Deal in the late 1930s and early 1940s brought a new source of funding for the Democrats: union funds. As unions grew, so did their support of Democratic candidates, with unions quickly becoming a major revenue source for the Democratic Party.[15] Congressional Republicans (along with southern Democrats, who were not receiving the union contributions) passed the War Labor Disputes Act of 1943 (a.k.a. the Smith-Connally Act), prohibiting unions from using their treasury funds as political contributions to federal candidates.[16] The bill was vetoed by President Roosevelt, but he was over ruled by a two-thirds vote of the Senate. But because the bill was passed as a war measure it was removed automatically as law six months after the war ended. The Labor Management Relations Act of 1947 (a.k.a. the Taft-Hartley Act) reinstated the provisions of the Smith-Connally Act.

Before World War II, "the political party served as the primary link between the people and their government."[17] Local party leaders were always available to take complaints or offer a helping hand. After World War II, however, civil servants began to take on many of the bureaucratic responsibilities once held by the local party. As a result, the party declined in importance among voters, and congressional campaigns shifted from a party-based effort to a candidate-based effort.[18] Candidates began taking over more and more responsibility for raising and spending their own funds.[19] Thus, Congress paid little attention to campaign finance reform.

During his speech to the Conference on Free TV and Political Reform, President Clinton credited President John Kennedy with originating the idea of implementing reform by providing free air time in 1962 (speech, March 11, 1997). Although it is not clear that the idea actually originated with Kennedy, he did at least visit the idea of campaign finance reform. Critics of Kennedy alleged that he "bought" his presidential election because of his father's pocketbook.[20] His wealth allegedly purchased not only media but political supporters as well. To counter the rumors, in 1961 Kennedy created the Campaign Finance Commission. This panel was charged with evaluating the financial climate of campaigns and making reform recommendations. In 1962, the panel presented a proposal that included limiting contributions, establishing public funds, and expanding disclosure.[21] Congress was not interested in reform, however, and simply ignored the recommendations.

In 1966, President Johnson had a bill introduced to revamp the 1925 federal Corrupt Practices Act.[22] Although Johnson's bill went nowhere, Congress did pass a major reform bill. Sponsored by Sen. Russell Long (D-LA), this bill created public funds for presidential elections by allowing voters a box to check on their tax form to allocate $1.00 to the "Presidential Election Campaign Fund." Amid much controversy, the bill passed (PL 89-809).[23]

The very next spring, however, Sen. Albert Gore (D-TN) and Sen. John Williams (R-DE) proposed an amendment to repeal the Long Act (PL 90-26). Congress eventually voted to postpone the provisions of the Act until more research could be done.[24]

## 1970s and 1980s

Real reform began to take shape in 1971. The Federal Election Campaign Act (FECA) was passed in 1971 and signed into law in 1972 by President Nixon.[25] This law tried to address the weaknesses of campaign finance reform that prior legislation had missed. In an attempt to stem the escalating costs of campaigning, the first part of the bill set a limit on how much money candidates could spend on media advertising and restricted the amount of money a candidate could contribute to his/her own campaign.[26] It also tightened up disclosure laws, restricted donations from corporations and unions, and set in motion the concept of volunteer political action committees (PACs). Reformers were convinced that real change was underway. Rep. Morris K. Udall (D-AZ) said, "We have a crackerjack bill here. It will stop millionaires from buying Senate seats and the Presidency. It brings this television monster under control."[27]

Then came Watergate. Unfolding from 1972 to 1974, the Watergate investigations drew attention from all parts of the country. Misused campaign funds were just one part of the scandal that eventually unseated President Nixon.[28] Ironically, the bill Nixon signed into law at the beginning of 1972 requiring full disclosure provided a paper trail for investigators to follow. In the wake of the scandal, in 1974 congress passed amendments strengthening FECA. Provisions returned the voluntary $1.00 tax donation check off box, greatly limited expenditures, and limited contributions to $1,000 per individual and $5,000 per PAC (per candidate, per election).[29] Candidates were required to limit personal contributions to their war chest, a move designed to keep the wealthy from buying seats.[30] This bill also established a governing body, the Federal Elections Commission (FEC), to oversee the new reforms. President Gerald Ford signed the act into law in 1974 (PL 93-443).

Reformers didn't celebrate long. In 1976, in *Buckley v. Valeo*, the Supreme Court ruled that limiting expenditures in an election was, in effect, limiting free speech for the candidate and was therefore a violation of the First Amendment. Additionally, the ruling struck down limits on how much money a candidate could invest in his/her own campaign. Justice Potter Stewart said, "We are talking about speech, money is speech and speech is money, whether it is buying television or radio time or newspaper advertising, or even buying pencils and paper and microphones."[31] The Justices upheld the limits on direct contributions to candidates, however.

In 1979 congress was still struggling to redefine the tenets of campaign finance law. At least two bills were presented on the topic (H. 1 and S. 832) but failed to make it through the legislative process. However, a bill designed to strengthen state parties was introduced and passed. The bill provided a way for political parties to raise funds to build the party. Drives to register voters or to remind voters of election day (commonly called "get out the vote" or "GOTV" drives) could be funded through party fundraising.[32] President Jimmy Carter signed the bill into law (PL 96-187) unintentionally opening the door for the "soft money" debates that rage today.

For most of the eighties, campaign finance reform was a dormant issue. By the end of the decade, however, several FEC rulings had escalated soft money into a powerful and even dominant campaign presence.[33] Finance reform again returned to the forefront of congressional discussions.

The "Free Political Broadcasting Act of 1985" was introduced by Rep. Samuel Stratton (D-NY) in January, 1987 (H.R. 521). This bill provided free air time for all congressional and presidential candidates in the 30 days before the general election. The amount of time was to be determined by the popular votes the candidate's party received in the most recent election and therefore favored the dominant parties. Seventy-five percent of the free time was required to be in prime time. There was no floor action on this bill.[34]

Rep. Andrew Jacobs introduced a bill in January, 1987, calling for public financing of advertising (H.R. 480). This included radio, television, newspapers, and other related expenses. The bill died in committee.[35]

In 1988, Sen. Robert C. Byrd (D-WVA), the Senate Majority Leader, "held a record-setting cloture vote in an attempt to bring to the floor legislation that would have set voluntary spending limits for Senate campaigns, offered public funds to candidates who abided by the limits and restricted PAC contributions."[36] Republican opponents, led by Sen. Mitch McConnell (R-KY), successfully stalled the bill to death.

The "Campaign Broadcast Discount Act of 1988" was introduced in July of 1988. Sponsored by Sen. McConnell, this bill offered deeply discounted air time, and required stations to allow candidates to purchase "fixed" time that could not be preempted (S. 2627). The bill was referred to committee where it died.[37]

Another bill that called for free airtime was introduced in October, 1988 by soon-to-be Vice President Al Gore, then a Senator from Tennessee.[38] This bill, the "Presidential Election Issues Access Act," called for the FCC to require each radio and television station to provide six and one-half hours of free air time to the presidential candidates from the Republican and Democrat parties (S. 2923). This time was to be provided only during the eight weeks before the general election. The bill was referred to committee, where it died.[39]

## REFORM IN THE 1990s

Between 1989 and 1991, congress was again wracked by scandal. The savings and loan (S&L) crisis was an unmitigated fiscal catastrophe for the American public. Added to that was the congressional and public dismay over the so-called Keating Five. The Keating Five were five Senators who protected a major contributor (an S&L director named Charles Keating) from federal regulators. Eventually, an investigation determined that Keating had been stealing from his S&L; Keating went to prison, but the Senators were not charged due to lack of evidence that they had "profited personally."[40]

While the Keating scandal raged, Senator William Roth introduced an untitled bill in August of 1990 (S. 2964). This bill provided free air time for all federal candidates but left the details to the discretion of the FCC. The bill stipulated that the time would be limited to personal appearances such as debates, speeches, etc.—no free time would be given for advertising. Candidates would also have to agree not to purchase any additional time if they took advantage of the free air time. This proposed bill, then, virtually eliminated political advertising and placed incumbents on the same level as challengers by giving both equal access to the electronic media. Incumbents, however, generally prefer to depend on their ability to build deep war chests; leveling the playing field is not in their best interest. Indeed, this bill was referred to committee where it died; there was no floor vote.[41]

New campaign finance reform bills finally passed both the House and Senate in 1992, partly in direct answer to the Keating scandal.[42] In the House, Rep. Samuel Gejdenson (D-CT) introduced the Campaign Spending Limit and Election Reform Act of 1991 (H.R. 3750). The House amended this bill to match its Senate version, the Senate Election Ethics Act of 1991 (S. 3), which was presented by Sen. David Boren (D-OK). Provisions of the bill (S. 3) included free television air time vouchers for the Senate and matching federal funds for House candidates. Boren's bill was approved by both branches of Congress, but President George Bush vetoed the measure. Congress was unable to override his veto.[43]

Reform bills passed both the House and Senate again in 1993. The bill introduced by Sen. Boren in the Senate (S.3) was also introduced by Rep. Gejdenson in the House (H.R. 3). The provisions lowered PAC contribution values and provided deeply discounted television time for Senate candidates. House candidates were to be provided with vouchers for advertising and postage. Soft money was to be banned. Although the bills initially passed, Republicans in the Senate filibustered and ultimately killed the Senate version. The Republican charge was led by Sen. Mitch McConnell.[44]

In 1996, a bipartisan coalition was formed to address campaign finance reform. Led by Sen. John McCain (R-AZ) and Sen. Russ Feingold (D-WI), the coalition's proposed bill eliminated PACs and soft money, encouraged voluntary spending limits, and provided free television time for candidates who choose to participate (S. 1219). Consideration of the bill continued as President Clinton re-emphasized the importance of these reforms for his Democratic agenda.

## MCCAIN-FEINGOLD

The 1996 McCain-Feingold campaign finance reform bill was titled the "Bipartisan Campaign Reform Act of 1997." This bill actually passed through committee and was placed on the calendar (S. 1219). This act sought to ban soft money contributions and set voluntary limits on campaign spending. Limits were also established for personal contributions of candidates as well as total expenditures. The Senate bill was presented to the floor but McCain-Feingold did not raise the 60 votes needed to bring the bill up for a vote. Although McCain didn't actually expect to win the first round, the Senator did vow that "the issue is not going away."[45]

McCain-Feingold was reintroduced in the Senate in 1997 (S. 25). Allowing the bill to be brought to the floor, Senate Majority Leader Trent Lott (R-MS) then threw the measure into disarray by proposing an amendment restricting contributions from union PACs.[46] Prompted by intense union spending against vulnerable Republican incumbents in the previous election, the amendment would have required labor unions to get permission from all their members before placing any dues into political action accounts.[47] Lott himself was strongly opposed to the McCain-Feingold bill; supporters of the bill were strongly opposed to Lott's amendment. Both procedures therefore ended in a stalemate, with neither side being able to collect enough votes to allow a roll call vote on either issue.

Meanwhile in the House, a companion bill to McCain-Feingold was introduced. Sponsored by Rep. Christopher Shays (R-CT) and Rep. Martin Meehan (D-MA), the Shays-Meehan bill addressed many of the same concerns the Senate was debating (H.R. 3526). The measure banned soft money, restricted party expenditures (but raised donation limits), and required labor unions to publicize PAC contributions to members. The Shays-Meehan bill passed the House by a vote of 252-179, but because the companion bill (McCain-Feingold) could not pass the Senate, Shays-Meehan did not become law.

McCain-Feingold reappeared on the floor of the Senate in February, 1998, then again in September, 1998, this time by attaching the measure to an appropriations bill (S. 2237). A motion to end debate failed by a vote of 52-48, effectively killing the bill; Sen. McCain withdrew his amendment but vowed, "We won't give up this fight."[48] But McCain-Feingold was pronounced "dead on revival" by Charles Pope, a reporter for *Congressional Quarterly Weekly*.[49]

In a letter to this author, Sen. John McCain explained his reasons for continuing to fight for campaign finance reform.

> At the time this legislation was introduced, the Congress was enjoying a whopping 19 percent approval rating. I felt it was my duty to do something to restore the public's confidence in the Congress as an institution. It was at that time, and still is, very clear to me that the only way to restore the public's faith in the Congress and the electoral system was by leveling the playing field between incumbents and challengers. It is still evident today that the best way this can be accomplished is by encouraging candidates to focus their campaigns on ideas and ideals, not on how much money they can raise and spend.[50]

In January 1999, the Shays-Meehan bill was reintroduced in the House (H.R. 417) and titled the "Bipartisan Campaign Reform Act of 1999."[51] Finally, after numerous revisions and modifications, the bills passed both chambers of Congress in March 2002. The Bipartisan Campaign Reform Act of 2002 (BCRA) banned the collection of unregulated soft money by national parties, raised the limits on contribution amounts by individuals to candidates for federal office, and set regulations on issue ads, called "electioneering communication." President Bush signed the bill into law on March 27, 2002, calling it an improvement, although "far from perfect." The BCRA is discussed in more detail in chapter 5, "The History of 527s."

## CAMPAIGN ECONOMICS

In politics, money is always the driving force. The nature of the political system requires candidate to raise and spend money in order to reach voters. Even the Supreme Court has ruled that, in politics, money is speech (*Buckley v. Valeo*, 1976). Campaign finance reformers often point out, however, that basic economic policies are violated in most campaign finance regulations. Through various congressional laws and Supreme Court rulings the United States has arrived at a funding set-up that "no rational legislator would ever have chosen,"[52] a plan that virtually ignores the basic economic theory of supply and demand.

To a politician, money equals access to voters. Campaign finance reform has focused on either regulating supply (money donated) or regulating demand (money spent).[53] Congress has yet to find the balance between regulating supply and regulating demand. Several critics lay the blame for the imbalance at the feet of the Supreme Court and the *Buckley v. Valeo* (1976) decision.[54] As discussed previously, *Buckley v. Valeo* overruled the idea of limiting expenditures (demand) in campaigns. Equating money with speech, this decision effectively ruled that spending limits are a type of censorship and are thereby unlawful under the first amendment. One critic called *Buckley v. Valeo* "a constitutional straitjacket that locks American democracy into the worst of all possible finance worlds."[55] For this reason, bills introduced since 1976 have sought ways to encourage candidates to *voluntarily* limit expenditures.

By the same token, this measure upheld the limit on contributions (supply). "Ask any economist what happens to a market in which demand is unlimited but supply is seriously constrained" demanded one critic.[56] In a goods market, this scenario increases the likelihood of products appearing on the black market. In the political arena, the imbalance has led candidates to develop more and more creative ways to circumvent the law and increase the supply. "Sheer pressure of demand will quickly find an inventive (read questionable) means of supply."[57] This is evidenced in the rise of "soft money" in campaigns despite repeated "bans"—and the continued shell game played by politicians.

## NOTES

1. Larry J. Sabato and G. R. Simpson, *Dirty Little Secrets: The Persistence of Corruption in American Politics* (New York: Random House, 1996); Anthony Corrado, "Money and Politics: A History of Federal Campaign Finance Law," in Anthony Corrado, Thomas E. Mann, Daniel R. Ortiz, Trevor Potter, and Frank J. Sorauf, *Cam-*

*paign Finance Reform: A Sourcebook* (Washington, D.C.: Brookings Institution Press, 1997), pp. 27–35.

2. Corrado, "Money and Politics."
3. Corrado, "Money and Politics."
4. Corrado, "Money and Politics."
5. Corrado, "Money and Politics."
6. Corrado, "Money and Politics."
7. *Newberry v. United States* (1921) 256 U.S. 232.
8. Corrado, "Money and Politics."
9. Sabato and Simpson, *Dirty Little Secrets.*
10. Corrado, "Money and Politics."
11. Sabato and Simpson, *Dirty Little Secrets;* Corrado, "Money and Politics."
12. Corrado, "Money and Politics."
13. Corrado, "Money and Politics."
14. Corrado, "Money and Politics."
15. Corrado, "Money and Politics."
16. Corrado, "Money and Politics."
17. Karen S. Johnson-Cartee and Gary A. Copeland, *Inside Political Campaigns: Theory and Practice* (Westport, CT: Praeger, 1997), p. 6.
18. Johnson-Cartee and Copeland, *Inside Political Campaigns.*
19. Corrado, "Money and Politics."
20. Jonathan D. Salant, "Despite Attempts, Loopholes in Law Remain Unplugged," *Congressional Quarterly Weekly*, 54, no. 46 (Nov. 16, 1996): pp. 3274–3275.
21. Salant, "Despite Attempts"; Corrado, "Money and Politics."
22. Salant, "Despite Attempts."
23. Salant, "Despite Attempts"; Corrado, "Money and Politics."
24. Corrado, "Money and Politics."
25. Salant, "Despite Attempts"; Corrado, "Money and Politics."
26. Salant, "Despite Attempts"; Corrado, "Money and Politics."
27. Salant, "Despite Attempts," p. 2374.
28. Sabato and Simpson, *Dirty Little Secrets.*
29. Sabato and Simpson, *Dirty Little Secrets.*
30. Sabato and Simpson, *Dirty Little Secrets.*
31. Thomas Fleming, "The Long, Stormy Marriage of Money and Politics . . . or Why in America Campaign-Finance Reform Never Succeeds," *American Heritage*, 49, no. 7 (Nov. 1998): p. 5.
32. Rebecca Carr, "As Soft Money Grows, so Does Controversy." *Congressional Quarterly Weekly*, 54, no. 46 (Nov. 16, 1996): pp. 3272–3273; Sabato and Simpson, *Dirty Little Secrets;* Salant, "Despite Attempts."
33. Corrado, "Money and Politics."
34. Congressional Bill Summary, THOMAS, a division of the Library of Congress, 1999. Accessed through the Library of Congress Web site http://thomas.loc.gov/home/thomas.html.
35. Congressional Bill Summary, 1999.
36. Salant, "Despite Attempts," p. 3275.
37. Congressional Bill Summary, 1999.

38. William J. Clinton, "Remarks by the President in Address to the Conference on Free TV and Political Reform," National Press Club, March 11, 1997.
39. Congressional Bill Summary, 1999.
40. Sabato and Simpson, *Dirty Little Secrets,* p. 9.
41. Congressional Bill Summary, 1999.
42. Salant, "Despite Attempts."
43. Salant, "Despite Attempts."
44. Salant, "Despite Attempts."
45. Salant, "Despite Attempts."
46. Carroll J. Doherty, "Votes a Good Indicator of Depth of Feelings on Both Sides," *Congressional Quarterly Weekly,* 55, no. 40 (Oct. 11, 1997): p. 2449.
47. Doherty, "Votes a Good Indicator."
48. Charles Pope, "McCain-Feingold Bill on Campaign Financing Proves Dead on Revival," *Congressional Quarterly Weekly,* 56, no. 36 (Sept. 12, 1998): p. 2402.
49. Pope, "McCain-Feingold."
50. John McCain, unpublished letter to the author, March 5, 1999.
51. Bipartisan Campaign Reform Act of 1997, S. 25 PCS, January 21, 1997.
52. "How to Cut the Cost of Politics," *The Economist,* 342, no. 8003 (Feb. 8, 1997): pp. 17–18.
53. Burt Neuborne, "One Dollar, One Vote?" *The Nation,* 263, no. 18 (Dec. 2, 1996): p. 22.
54. "Politicians for Rent," *The Economist,* 342, no. 8003 (Feb. 8, 1997): pp. 23–25; Neuborne, "One Dollar, One Vote."
55. Neuborne, "One Dollar, One Vote."
56. Neuborne, "One Dollar, One Vote."
57. "Politicians for Rent."

## LEGISLATIVE CITATIONS

H.R. 417, 106th Cong., 1st Sess. (1999).
H.R. 1400, 103rd Cong., 1st Sess. (1993).
H.R. 3, 103rd Cong., 1st Sess. (1993).
H.R. 3750, 102d Cong., 1st Sess. (1991).
H.R. 480, 100th Cong., 1st Sess. (1987).
H.R. 521, 100th Cong., 1st Sess. (1987).
H.R. 5010, 96th Cong., 1st Sess. (1979). Public Law 96-187 (01/08/80)S. 25, 105th Cong., 1st Sess. (1997).
S. 652, 104th Cong., 1st Sess. (1995). Public Law 104-104 (02/08/96).
S. 3, 102d Cong., 1st Sess. (1991). Revised 4/8/92.
S.2964, 101st Cong., 2nd Sess. (1990).
S. 2627, 100th Cong., 2d Sess. (1988).
S.2627, 100th Cong., 2d. Sess. (1988).

## BIBLIOGRAPHY

Bipartisan Campaign Reform Act of 1997, S. 25 PCS, January 21, 1997.

Carr, Rebecca. "As Soft Money Grows, so Does Controversy." *Congressional Quarterly Weekly*, 54, no. 46 (Nov. 16, 1996): pp. 3272–73.

Clinton, William J. "Remarks by the President in Address to the Conference on Free TV and Political Reform." The National Press Club, March 11, 1997.

Congressional Bill Summary, THOMAS, a division of the Library of Congress, 1999. Accessed through the Library of Congress Web site http://thomas.loc.gov/home/thomas.html.

Corrado, Anthony. "Money and Politics: A History of Federal Campaign Finance Law." In Anthony Corrado, Thomas E. Mann, Daniel R. Ortiz, Trevor Potter, and Frank J. Sorauf, *Campaign Finance Reform: A Sourcebook* (Washington, D.C.: Brookings Institution Press, 1997), pp. 27–35.

Doherty, Carroll J. "Votes a Good Indicator of Depth of Feelings on Both Sides." *Congressional Quarterly Weekly*, 55, no. 40 (Oct. 11, 1997): p. 2449.

Fleming, Thomas. "The Long, Stormy Marriage of Money and Politics . . . or Why in America Campaign-Finance Reform Never Succeeds." *American Heritage*, 49, no. 7 (Nov. 1998).

"How to Cut the Cost of Politics," *The Economist*, 342, no. 8003 (Feb. 8, 1997): pp. 17–18.

Johnson-Cartee, Karen S., and Gary A. Copeland. *Inside Political Campaigns: Theory and Practice* (Westport, CT: Praeger, 1997).

Neuborne, Burt. "One Dollar, One Vote?" *The Nation*, 263, no. 18 (Dec. 2, 1996): p. 22.

"Politicians for Rent," *The Economist*, 342, no. 8003 (Feb. 8, 1997): pp. 23–25.

Pope, Charles. "McCain-Feingold Bill on Campaign Financing Proves Dead on Revival," *Congressional Quarterly Weekly*, 56, no. 36 (Sept. 12, 1998): p. 2402.

Sabato, Larry J., and G. R. Simpson. *Dirty Little Secrets: The Persistence of Corruption in American Politics* (New York: Random House, 1996).

Salant, Jonathan D. "Despite Attempts, Loopholes in Law Remain Unplugged." *Congressional Quarterly Weekly*, 54, no. 46 (Nov. 16, 1996): pp. 3274–3275.

# 2

# Political Parties and the Finance Law

*Larry Powell*

Political parties, like political candidates, are also subject to campaign finance laws. While candidates raise money for their campaign efforts, a dual fundraising effort occurs at the same time by the political parties. Political parties—both Democrats and Republicans—need funds to maintain the annual activities of their groups. But they also use campaigns as an impetus for raising funds that are then used to assist in partisan campaign efforts. This soft money is then used to promote party activities. Sometimes it is also used to circumvent the rules and is targeted toward messages that aid specific candidates.

Either way, campaign finance laws have served to increase the role of the political parties in campaigns. Both parties have adapted their techniques in light of changes in the law brought on by the McCain-Feingold Act. That law was the latest in several relevant changes since the 1970s. La Raja argued that such legislation has had a positive impact on political parties, arguing that "Money strengthens the independent role of parties in elections."[1] He further outlined that the cumulative effect of these changes has led to four distinct changes in the relationship of the parties and their candidates: (1) the party organization started to assume a larger role in campaigns; (2) party financing became centralized at the national level; (3) that increase in money provided more influence for the national parties; and (4) —primarily as a result of the Bipartisan Campaign Reform Act (BCRA) of 2002—the parties increased their efforts to raise money from small donors through direct mail and the Internet.

## THE NATIONAL COMMITTEES

Each major political party has a national committee that oversees the party's political activities, including (1) organizing the party's national convention, (2) developing its political platform, (3) coordination of campaign strategies, and (4) fundraising. The national committees also work with state committees and coordinates activities with their respective legislative committees for Senate and congressional campaigns. Still, most of the money allocated for local contests are in marginal races that are seen as competitive by both sides.[2]

The Democratic National Committee (DNC) was founded in 1848 at the party's national convention. The Democratic Congressional Campaign Committee (DCCC) was established 12 years later in 1866. The Republican National Committee (RNC) was founded in 1856 (two years after the organization of the modern Republican Party) to aid in the unsuccessful campaign of John C. Fremont, its first presidential nominee. The National Republican Congressional Committee (NRCC), organized in 1866, works for candidates to the House of Representatives. The senate committee was organized in 1916 following the ratification of the 17th Amendment, which provided the first direct election of senators.[3]

### Candidate Party vs. Party Money

Funds for political activities can be donated either to a candidate or to political party. Prior to 2002, both national parties operated under a system that divided campaign contributions into "hard money" and "soft money"

*Hard Money vs. Soft Money.* Hard money is the designation used for donations made to the candidate or the campaign; hard money is subject to the restrictions of the campaign finance laws. Under those rules, when the campaign is actively engaged in activities aimed at seeking voter support or actively requests that voters vote against a specific other candidate, it is required to spend hard money on those efforts.

Soft money are funds given by corporations, labor unions and wealthy individuals to the party.[4] Soft money was not regulated and could be given in unlimited amounts. It was supposed to be used only for get-out-the-vote and other general political activities and not to promote specific candidates for federal office. Often it was used to do just that—by coming just short of using forbidden words, such as "vote for" or "vote against." Such leniency in the regulations was one reason that Mann argued that party soft money "has created as many or more problems for parties and done little to nurture grass roots participation or electoral competition."[5]

For example, one of the most open uses of soft money during the 2000 elections came from the Virginia-based Republican Majority Issues Committee, which sought to raise $25 million in donations that ranged from $500,000 to $3 million while promising its donors that they would remain anonymous. Such an approach was legal, provided (1) neither the group nor its ads explicitly tell voters which candidates to vote for or against, (2) the committee received no guidance from Republican congressional or party leaders, and (3) it did not coordinate its efforts with any of the candidates it supports. If a group met those three requirements, it was not required to register with the Federal Election Commission and, as a result, not required to report its donors nor limit the size of donations from individuals. In addition, corporate donations were also legal. As a result, the soft money angle provided a means for corporate America to funnel millions of dollars into the coffers of political parties.[6] This factor resulted in criticism of the law as providing such corporations with too much influence in the electoral process.[7]

A key element in the "soft money" regulations was that there were few limits as to how much any one entity could contribute. That changed in 2002 under the Bipartisan Campaign Reform Act. Part of that act was to "ban" the use of soft money. Individuals could still donate to the parties, but contributions were capped at $28,500 to party committees.[8] Pragmatically, that $28,500 limitation had no major impact on the parties' fundraising efforts. Prior to that date, 90 percent of soft money contributors gave less than $25,000, and the average contribution was only $8,750.[9]

The Bipartisan Campaign Reform Act of 2003 tried to eliminate the use of soft money by the national parties by placing the parties under the same hard money requirements that regulated campaigns. Still, many campaigns continued to use the national parties as a means of paying their campaign staffs. Further, state parties could still collect soft money funds. Under a compromise agreement, state and local party organizations can collect an unlimited amount of "Levin funds" from corporations, labor unions and individuals—up to a maximum of $10,000 from each contributor.[10] This money faces the same type of spending limitations that were required by the old "soft money" rules, for example, the funds can only be used for voter registration and get-out-the-vote activities during federal elections.

Further, donations to independent groups have few limits.[11] Thus observers of the changes brought by the BCRA quickly predicted that the new law would benefit independent groups.[12] Indeed, analysis of advertising spending after the 2004 election identified few differences in campaign expenditures,[13] but independent groups became more important. For example, in the 2004 election, Texas millionaire Boone Pickens donated millions of dollars to the Swift Boat Veterans for Truth, a 527 group that Republicans used to attack John Kerry.[14]

## RULES OF THE GAME

Candidates cannot merely enter a campaign and immediately start to raise and spend money. Modern campaigns play by a sophisticated, complicated and often confusing set of rules. Federal candidates (Presidents, senators, congressmen) must adhere to federal laws that are monitored by the Federal Elections Commission (FEC). State and local candidates have a different set of rules, although many of those local regulations are patterned after the federal guidelines. Although there are some exceptions for local regulations, the relevant laws generally fall into three different categories—limitations on contributions, reporting requirements, and limitations on spending.

*Campaign Contributions.* Federal law limits contributions for federal elections—campaigns for president, U.S. senator or U.S. Congressmen—initially set at $1,000 for individuals and raised to $2,300 in 2003. That limit was raised to $2,400 for the 2010 election cycle.[15] Once any election is completed, the contributor can donate again for the next election. The implication of this factor is that, for some candidates, the actual ceiling on individual contributions for one elections cycle is $7,200, not $2,400. A contributor could donate $2,400 to the candidate's primary campaign, a similar donation to the primary run-off, and still make a third donation to the general election.

Finally, the financial books close on each of the phases except in one important respect. Funds may be raised for a primary or runoff or general election to the extent of debt. If a campaign owes money at the end of and of these periods, it may continue to raise money to pay off that debt. Often a financial contributor of a beaten opponent will contribute to a winner by helping to raise funds to pay off earlier debts. In 2008, after Barack Obama defeated Hillary Clinton for the Democratic presidential nomination, Obama called on his contributors to help Clinton pay off her debt—and contribution $2,300 himself for that purpose.[16] Potential contributors who might not want their support known might pledge a later contribution to pay off debt. The same contributors may then contribute in subsequent phases of the campaign.

The goal of contribution limits is to make campaigns more "democratic," for example, the result of the election will be based on the candidates and their campaigns rather than a byproduct of one's ability to raise money. Some research has suggested that campaign contribution limits do indeed contribute to a more democratic process.[17] Others take the opposite position, arguing that the main effect of campaign finance laws has been to increase the re-election of incumbents and to limit the viability of challengers.[18] Pragmatically, it may make little difference. In 2008, Barack Obama was successful in raising significant funds from small donors for his presidential campaign, but the prospects of similar success for either of the national party is considerably more pessimistic. As Cotter and Hennessy once noted, because of a variety of factors, "the national committees cannot hope to be supported soon, or perhaps ever, entirely by small donations."[19]

*Reporting Requirements.* To monitor and enforce campaign contribution laws, both the federal and state governments rely primarily on specific reporting requirements. Reporting requirements are typically strict, even those elections that are not subject to limitations on contributions. For that reason, most major campaigns employ both a lawyer and an accountant to make sure that the "books" are in proper shape and that all reports are made in a timely manner.

Keeping those books requires a sophisticated set of records. In federal elections, for example, the $2,400 dollar limit is cumulative for each individual campaign. A contributor who donates $1,000 early in the campaign, can later donate $1,400 more, but not more than that. When a contributor reaches a cumulative total of $2,400, they have "maxed out" for that election and not allowed to contribute further. Thus, the campaign's accounting system must be sufficiently complex to keep up with individual contributions and the cumulative total of each individual's contributions.

*Spending Limitations.* The goal of spending limitations is to create a more level playing field for candidates. Ideally, the winner of the election should be the candidate with the best ideas, not the one with the most money, and spending limitations are an attempt to provide more parity on this front. However, neither the federal nor local governments may unilaterally limit expenditures for all candidates. Candidates may spend their own funds without limits. In *FEC v. Buckley*, the Supreme Court held that doing so would be to interfere with those candidates' right to freedom of speech.

This "free speech" argument is the key to opponents of campaign finance reform[20]—particularly among Republicans, who are more likely to oppose constraints on political money.[21] In fact, opponents find offense in the phrase "campaign reform" itself. As Ari Fleischer, former press secretary for President George W. Bush, once commented, "Why do the press label the debate over campaign finance reform as a matter of 'reform,' not 'speech rights.'"[22] Similarly, *Washington Post* columnist George Will argued that reform laws were unconstitutional because a third party group "is another organization by which people *assemble* to *speak* in order to seek *redress of grievances.*"[23] On another occasion, he specifically criticized the McCain-Feingold law (BRCA) as "abridging freedom of political speech" because "it restricts the quantity, timing and content of such speech."[24]

Balancing those conflicting tensions is an issue that is still being addressed by the courts.[25] As a result, spending limitations can only be placed on those candidates who choose to raise their funds or, in the case of presidential campaigns those who accept matching funds from the government.

If the candidate accepts governmental funds, or otherwise chooses not to use personal funds then the government has the right to place rules on how those funds are spent.

Congressional and senatorial candidates are typically not eligible for matching campaign funds, unless they qualify under regulations for their individual states. As such, there are rarely any spending limits for those types of races, only the individual contributions limits. For presidential candidates who choose matching funds, the first $250 of each individual contribution can be matched by federal funds.

In the 2000 presidential primary campaign, for example, candidates who accepted matching money were limited to spending $40.5 million during the primary campaigns (that amount varies with each election). If the candidate chose not to accept matching money, they were not bound by any spending limits. During the 2000 election, Republican George W. Bush raised more than $70 million in individual and PAC contributions; he chose not to accept federal matching funds and spent much of that total during the primary season. Meanwhile, Democrat Al Gore accepted federal funds and was limited to the $40.5 million ceiling on primary expenditures. Similarly, in the 2008 election, Democrat Barack Obama chose not to accept federal funds, while Republican John McCain took the money.

In presidential elections, the general election campaign officially begins after the parties formally nominate candidates at their conventions in August. That portion of the presidential campaign is funded by taxpayers. In 2000, the Democratic and Republican candidates each got $67.5 million, and both were prohibited from using other funds. Theoretically, a candidate could refuse the federal money and raise money under the same rules as for the primaries.

The bottom line for the consultant is that they must become familiar with the local laws as quickly as possible. Not surprisingly, the most valuable volunteers the campaign can recruit are local lawyers and accountants who are willing to research the legal aspects of the campaign.

## CIRCUMVENTING THE RULES

In 2002, Congress was still working on the McCain-Feingold Bipartisan Campaign Reform Act when observant politicos spotted loopholes in the law.[26] That applies to nearly all efforts to regulate campaign ethics. The basic regulations provide only a broad framework for the legal side of campaign finances. Campaigns often look for ways to adhere to the letter of the law while expanding the amount of money they are legally allowed to raise and spend. A number of avenues have been used for this purpose.

*Soft Money Expenditures.* The most common method for circumventing the rules is through the distinction between "hard money" and "soft money," with the parties' taking advantage of loopholes regarding the expenditure of soft money. Campaign finance laws place no spending limits or fundraising limits on soft money. The only limitations on "soft money" why it is spent. Soft money is viewed as the party's money, not that of the candidate. Thus soft money can be used to promote party activities and party views, but it is not supposed to be used to actively solicit votes for any specific candidate. In essence, such ads will say "Congressman X is one of us. He supports us with his vote by opposing abortion on demand and gun control. He supports us in the U.S. House of Representatives." A hard money ad will say, "Congressman X is one of us. He supports us with his vote by opposing abortion on demand and gun control. Vote for X and keep him in the U.S. House of Representatives." The campaigns thus walk a fine line adhering to those requirements while maximizing expenditures. Some of the techniques they use include:

- *Staff Transfers.* Once a candidate has received the party's nomination, they typically shift most of the campaign staff to the party headquarters. That allows campaign workers to continue to draw regular paychecks without any of the funds counting against the "hard money" spending limitations of the campaign. Those expenditures still count against the hard money funds of the national party, but individuals can be placed on state party payrolls and be paid with soft money.
- *Consulting Services.* Many consulting services are not consider to be direct efforts to solicit votes. Polling is considered a form of research that is separate from the advertising efforts. Voter turnout programs can be organized to help all of the party's candidates, not just individual candidates. Consequently, payment for such services can come from the party, thus giving the campaign more room to operate under the spending limits. As Democratic turnout consultant Gerry Tyson noted, "As long as hard dollars are used, . . . the campaigns and party organizations seem to be on equal footing."[27]
- *Issue Ads.* While soft money was—theoretically—not supposed to be used for campaign ads, prior to the BCRA, both parties frequently did so under the guise of "issue ads."[28] Issue ads were legal; both parties had the right to communicate their position on issues that they deem important. To be within the legal guidelines, however, the ads could not solicit voter support for a candidate. Typically, the parties got around this requirement by simply using the issue ad to address a campaign theme deemed important by the campaign, and then merely omitting the traditional "Vote for Candidate X" line at the end of the ad. The first major use of issue ads came during the 1996 presidential

campaign when both Bill Clinton and Bob Dole used their national party organizations to buy millions of dollars worth of TV spots. The Clinton ads, paid for by Democratic National Committee ran almost continuously for more than twelve months before the election in key markets and totaled more than $46 million dollars; the Republicans joined the fray later and spent a similar amount.

- *Voter Turnout.* Parties are allowed to use soft money for voter turnout efforts, for example, getting their voters to the polls. These efforts have been a staple of party politics for some time, particularly at the state and local level. The McCain-Feingold legislation (BRCA) limited state parties to $10,000 donations for turnout efforts.[29] As a result, by 2004, both parties were sending more money to state parties for such efforts.[30] Theoretically, such funds are intended for "party building," not campaigning. Realistically, though, "soft money regularly shows up in coordinated campaigns for candidates in which state, local, and national parties cooperate and comingle their funds."[31] As a result, as Hrebenar, Benedict and Burbank noted, one "indicator of the parties' electoral impact is their ability to increase the proportion of money going to the coordinated and independent expenditures categories."[32]
- *Independent Expenditures.* Despite the limitations on campaign donations and expenditures, most court decisions have interpreted the Freedom of Speech principle to mean that the government cannot limit the political activity of groups who wish to participate in the political process *as long as the group's activities are not coordinated with those of a campaign.* As a result, starting in the late 1970s, the involvement of friendly interest groups in campaigns has increased dramatically. The amount of money spent on such campaigns has increased, even as research indicated that it had little impact on voter choice or turnout.[33]

Kitchens and Powell reported on early third party campaigns by New Right organizations on behalf of Republican candidates,[34] a topic that will be addressed in the next chapter. Since then, as Drinkard, "They have grown more active with phone banks and ads that praise candidates who agree with them and rap those who don't."[35] The 2000 campaigns saw such activities on behalf of candidates from both parties. The AFL-CIO, the Sierra Club environmental organization and several abortion-rights groups spent millions to help democratic candidates, while the National Right to Life Committee, the Republican Leadership Council, Americans for Tax Reform and several other groups did the same for Republicans.

Despite the laxity in the rules, some groups occasionally get caught violating the law. During the 2004 campaign, a group called the Progress for America Voter Fund was fined $750,000—the third largest fine in FEC history—for circumventing donation laws.[36] The group spent $26.4 million on behalf of President Bush's re-election campaign in 11 battleground states. It's most memorable ad was called "Ashley's Story" and featured the President hugging a child whose mother had died in the 9/11 attacks on the World Trade Center. The ad was obviously intended to support the Bush campaign, but it adhered to the general rules and thus did not violate the "independent expenditure" component of the law. Instead, its legal problems came from not registering as a political action committee prior to airing the ads. As a PAC, it would have been subject to limits on campaign donations.

Bundling limits on campaign contributions are intended to limit the influence that any contributor can have on a candidate. Still, the relatively low ceiling on contribution limits makes it impossible for candidates to seek such contributions individually. Candidates handle that problem, and simultaneously circumvent the system, but creating a group of super contributors known as "bundlers." These contributors are asked to provide "bundles" of campaign contributions that include their own contributions, contributions from family members, and contributions from other associates. In the 2000 presidential election, for example, George W. Bush raised more than $70 million for his primary campaign, with much of that money raised by two-hundred bundlers known in the Bush camp as "Pioneers."[37] Similarly, in the 2008 campaign, John McCain had two sets of super-fundraisers—"Trailblazers" who raised at minimum of $100,000 each, and "Innovators" who raised a minimum of $250,000.[38] Legally, there is nothing wrong with this tactic, but it nullifies the law's intent to limit contributor influence.

There is, in fact, no legal requirement for the campaigns to identify who their bundlers are, and the process has been supported by the courts.[39] Several watchdog groups—including the Center for Responsive Politics, the Campaign Finance Institute, Common Cause, Democracy 21, the League of Women Voters, Public Citizen, and the Sunlight Foundation—have called on candidates to release information on their bundlers that include their names, the amount each raised, and some demographic information such as ZIP codes.[40] Still, the decision to do so is up to the campaigns.

## STATE PARTIES

The impetus for campaign finance reform at the national level has been mirrored by similar efforts within the states.[41] The result has been the development of multiple attempts at reform to make state campaigns more competitive.[42] Some of the resulting regulations reflect national policies while others are distinct to specific states.[43] Here are a few of the types of rules that campaigns must face at the state level.

*Multi-pack Ads.* In 1994, Florida Commissioner of Agriculture Bob Crawford seemed poised to easily win re-election to his low-profile state cabinet position. The Democrat had gradually built up a strong war chest while in office, and his Republican opponent was a relatively unknown candidate with little financial support. All that changed after the August party primaries. Jim Smith, the former Florida Attorney General, lost his bid for the Republican nomination for Governor. Following the loss, the Florida Republican Party announced that Smith would replace the unknown candidate on the ballot against Crawford. Overnight, Crawford had a well funded opponent whose name recognition exceeded his own. Crawford's research team soon realized that the (1) the Republican ploy was not popular with voters, but (2) it had occurred on a campaign so far down the ballot that most voters were not aware that a candidate switch had occurred.

The Crawford campaign concluded that they could win the campaign if they could get their message out, but one problem stood in the way. Television stations in the Orlando area were refusing to take campaign ads for the race. The campaign for Commissioner of Agriculture, they argued, was simply too far down the ballot to warrant TV time during a hectic election year. Tracking polls for the Crawford campaign showed that they were doing well in those markets where they could get on the air, but trailing badly to the better known Republican in the Orlando area. And, they conceded, there was little they could do about it.

That changed two weeks out from election day when the Florida Republican Party ran a series of ads for another party candidate. The ads fell under Florida's "six-pack" law, a ruling that allowed political parties to pay for election ads that were not limited to promoting the campaign of one candidate. In the "six-pack" version of the law, the ad must advocate the election of six different party candidates.

Both parties used the approach to get more air time for major candidates. The ads typically took the form of twenty-five seconds devoted to the candidate in a tight race, while five seconds was spent saying "also vote for these other five candidates." In this case, though, one of the other candidates mentioned was Republican Jim Smith.

The Crawford campaign quickly filed complaints with the Orlando television stations. The campaign argued that since the stations had broadcast ads promoting Smith's candidacy, the Crawford campaign should have access to equal time. After a review, all the stations agreed and sold a comparable amount of time to the Crawford campaign.

The resulting ads, detailing the candidate switch in the campaign, quickly raised awareness of the controversy in the Orlando area and gave the Crawford campaign the needed margin of victory. As one consultant for the Crawford campaign later said of the Republicans, "They had us beat and there was nothing we could do about it. And then they made that mistake."

The incident reflected several important elements about the role of political parties in state campaigns. Many states have individual laws that limit campaign activities and/or allow for ways of circumventing the campaign laws. The purpose of the "six-pack" law, and its cousin the "three-pack," was to encourage party fundraising to promote overall party activities. Essentially, the multi-pack laws are regulations that allow for soft money to be used for candidate advertisements as long as more than one candidate is depicted in each ad.

The regulations vary, but a typical requirement is for a "three-pack," for example, at least three different candidates must be mentioned in the ad. The intent of such regulations was to allow party advertisements that argue for the election of a partisan "team" of candidates, but both parties have used the law to support individual candidates. Candidates quickly learned to use it to get around fundraising limits, using the ads in a thinly disguised manner to raise soft money for their campaigns. The technique is simple, as reflected in the above example. The thirty-second ad is designed with twenty-five seconds devoted to the targeted candidate; the names and postage stamp-sized photos of two other candidates (sometimes candidates who have no opposition) are flashed during the final four seconds to make the ad a legal use of soft money. But its boomerang effect in the commissioner of agriculture campaign illustrated the potential unanticipated effects of its use.

Both issue ads and multi-pack ads skirt the intent of the original law, but the candidates generally go unpunished because of the ambiguity of the amended later versions of laws. In 1998, auditors at the Federal Election Commission ruled that both Clinton and Dole had exceeded their spending limits by using the soft money ads, but the Commission decided not to pursue enforcement because of the vagueness of the legislative requirements.[44] The practical effect of that decision was to give the presidential candidates of both parties almost total control of the budgets for their party's organization.

*State Parties as Expenditure Committees for Primary Campaigns.* A law that affected the 2006 campaigns in Florida was one that allowed political parties to spend soft money on behalf of primary candidates. This law marked a sharp shift in the regulations of independent expenditures in that it allowed the parties to get involved in campaign efforts before their nominee was selected. If fact, it went further than that. Theoretically, it allowed the party to help participate in the selection of the nominee.

The law worked liked this. Suppose a candidate had received contributions from wealthy contributors and had received the maximum contributions that those individual could donate to the campaign. That candidate would then request that those donors send additional contributions to his state party, designating the donations for independent expenditures for the campaigns. The party would collect the money, take a 15 percent handling fee for the party, and then used the remainder as independent expenditures for the candidate.

Three anomalies resulted from this arrangement. First, it put the parties in an unusual situation of potentially making independent expenditures on behalf of opposing candidates. For example, if two Republican candidates for the same congressional nomination used this indirect fundraising approach, the Florida Republican Party would be obligated to conduct independent expenditures for both candidates simultaneously.

This possibility led to the second anomaly in the law. The law eliminated the "independent" requirement of the independent expenditure. Specifically, to ensure that both candidates felt they were treated fairly in this process, both candidates were allowed to be involved in development of the advertising messages for these campaigns. The result: campaigns used the same consultants for both campaigns—their own in-house campaign plus the party's independent expenditure campaign.

Pragmatically, the law became a fundraising technique for the party. Regardless of which candidate won, the party would profit by taking a 15 percent share of the funds raised. However, it was also another way of circumventing both donation and expenditure rules—with no pretense of independence in terms of the activity.

The third anomaly of the law is that it increased the power of big-money players on political campaigns. In Florida, the industry which has been most active in contributing to campaigns has been that of the sugar industry, the group that Roberts labeled "the feudal lords of sugar."[45] This law gave such groups more power in Florida politics. Other states also have found ways of "collecting huge sums of money from wealthy individuals and interest groups and giving the money to gubernatorial and state legislative campaigns. In twenty-six states, money given by parties to candidates is not limited."[46] That approach allows candidates to get around contribution limits to their campaigns.[47]

Finally, state party organizations have been used to promote the campaigns of federal candidates for congressional and senate campaigns.[48] The major role of the state parties in such campaign is to provide organizational and voter turnout efforts, but as Brox noted, state parties are also in a position to provide campaign contributions to the candidates. They can also provide other services typically viewed as the job of the national party.

*Independent Groups*. The 527 groups active in federal election have their siblings in state elections, although the details vary from state to state. In the Florida model, allows a "committee of continuous existence" that all office holder have. There are no contribution limits for these groups, as long as they don't openly "advocate" for the candidate. However, these groups can pay for polling, consultant fees, and ad production. Further, they only have to file a report once a year, in December. That means that identification of the donors is often delayed until it's too late to have an impact on the election. As political pollster Jim Kitchens noted, "all the money starting in January will not be seen until after the election."[49]

*Reform Efforts.* Efforts at campaign reform at the state level face the same obstacles as those at the federal level. In 2007, New York's governor attempted to place contribution limits on state candidates.[50] The proposal also included a "millionaire's amendment" that kicked in if any candidate gave more than 20 times the contribution limit to their own campaign. In that case, opponents would be allowed to exceed donation limits for their own campaign. The plan also called for a $50,000 limit on the "housekeeping" accounts of state parties that were used for voter turnout programs. The proposal was killed by Republicans who suggested that the plan would help rich candidates, but the real issues seemed to be aspects of the bill that would have limited corporate contributions.

## SUMMARY

Campaign funds are raised amid a set of rules that govern campaign contributions, reporting, and spending limitations, but campaigns often use "soft" money to circumvent at least some of these requirements—particularly at the state level. State laws regarding party involvement vary on a state-by-state basis, but tend to follow the same trends as the laws at the federal level. What will differ, however, are the specifics of what is allowed and what is not allowed. Sometimes these make for unusual campaign scenarios, as in Florida where the law allows the party simultaneously to make independent expenditures for opposing candidates.

Overall, though, the financial side of political communication is full of potential ethical and legal potholes that can create problems for the candidate, the campaign, the donors, and the voters. Attempts to change the law are examined in detail by both of the major parties, with each side reluctant to support reform unless "it will give their party or faction an advantage over rivals." When reform legislation is passed, it is frequently in response to a specific scandal or salient issue. Even when the law is changed, however, partisan lawyers go through the revisions to find loopholes that the party can use to enhance the chances of electoral success for their candidates.

## NOTES

1. Raymond J. La Raja, *Small Change: Money, Political Parties, and Campaign Finance Reform* (Ann Arbor: University of Michigan Press, 2008), p. 209.

2. David F. Damore and Thomas G. Hansford, "The Allocation of Party Controlled Campaign Resources in the House of Representatives, 1989–1996," *Political Research Quarterly*, 53 (1999): 371–85.

3. Larry Powell, "Republican National Committee," in Linda Lee Kaid & C. Holtz-Bach (eds.), *Encyclopedia of Political Communication*, Vol. 2. (Los Angeles: Sage, 2008), pp. 711–12.

4. Adam Winkler, "Other People's Money: Corporations, Agency Costs, and Campaign Finance Law," *Georgetown Law Journal*, 92 (2004): 871–940.

5. Thomas E. Mann. "The Rise of Soft Money," in Anthony Corrado, Thomas E. Mann, & Trevor Potter (eds.), *Inside the Campaign Finance Battle* (Washington, DC: Brookings Institution Press, 2003), p. 32.

6. Mark Green, *Selling Out: How Big Corporate Money Buys Elections, Rams through Legislation, and Betrays Our Democracy* (New York: Regan Books, 2002).

7. Bradley A. Smith, *Unfree Speech: The Folly of Campaign Finance Reform* (Princeton: Princeton University Press, 2001).

8. Leslie Wayne, "A Spotlight on Bundling," *New York Times* (June 28, 2008), A10.

9. La Raja, *Small Change.*

10. Michael J. Malbin, *Life after Reform. When the Bipartisan Campaign Reform Act . . . Meets Politics* (Lanham, MD: Rowman & Littlefield, 2003).

11. Thomas Gais, *Improper Influence: Campaign Finance Law, Political Interest Groups, and the Problem of Equality* (Ann Arbor: University of Michigan Press, 1996).

12. Thomas B. Edsall, "Fundraising Specialists, Independent Groups Gain," *Washington Post* (December 11, 2003), p. A29.

13. Michael M. Franz, Joel Rivlin, and Kenneth Goldstein, "Much More of the Same: Television Advertising pre- and post-BRCA," in Michael J. Malbin (ed.), *The Election After Reform: Money, Politics, and the Bipartisan Campaign Reform Act* (Lanham, MD: Rowman and Littlefield, 2006), pp. 141–160.

14. Kate Zernike, "Veterans Rebut 'Swift Boat' Charges Against Kerry in Answer to Challenge," *New York Times*, (June 21, 2008), p. A17.

15. Lindsay Renick Mayer, "FEC Increases Campaign Contribution Limits," *Capital Eye Blog* (January 23, 2009), http://www.opensecrets.org/news/2009/01/fec-increases-campaign-contrib.html.

16. Jeff Zeleny, "Obama Gives $2,300, Intended as a Spur, for Clinton Debt," *New York Times* (June 27, 2008), p. A14.

17. Eom Kihong, and David A. Gross, "Democratization Effects of Campaign Contribution Limits in Gubernatorial Elections," *Party Politics*, 13 (2007): 695–720.

18. Smith, *Unfree Speech.*

19. Cornelius P. Cotter and Bernard C. Hennessy, *Politics without Power: The National Party Committees* (New York: Atherton, 1964), p. 186.

20. Melvin I. Urofsky, *Money and Free Speech: Campaign Finance Reform and the Courts* (Lawrence: University Press of Kansas, 2005); John Curtis Samples.

*The Fallacy of Campaign Finance Reform* (Chicago: University of Chicago Press, 2007).

21. J. Tobin Grant and Thomas J. Rudolph, *Expression vs. Equality: The Politics of Campaign Finance Reform* (Columbus: Ohio State University Press, 2004).

22. Ari Fleischer, *Taking Heat: The President, the Press, and My Years in the White House* (New York: William Morrow, 2005), p. 115.

23. George Will, "A Retreat on Rationing Free Speech," *Washington Post* (December 31, 2006): B7.

24. George Will, "McCain's Day of Repudiation," *Washington Post* (June 27, 2008), A17.

25. Tom DeLuca, "Free Speech, Political Equality, and Campaign Finance Reform: A Paradox for Democracy?" *New Political Science,* 29, no. 2 (2007): 145–166.

26. Richard A. Oppel Jr., "Sponsors Assert Soft Money Ban May Be Diluted," *New York Times* (June 14, 2002), A1.

27. Gerry Tyson, e-mail to the author (Dec. 2009).

28. David B. Magleby and J. Quin Monson, (eds.), *The Last Hurrah? Soft Money and Issue Advocacy in the 2002 Congressional Elections* (Washington, DC: Brookings Institution Press, 2002).

29. Jim Drinkard, "Some Win, Some Lose with Changes," *USA Today* (March 19, 2002), 2A.

30. Glen Justice, "Following New Rules, Parties Steer Money to the States," *New York Times,* (August 9, 2004), A24; Diana Dwyre and Robin Kolodny, "The Parties' Congressional Campaign Committees in 2004," in Michael J. Malbin (ed.), *The Election After Reform: Money, Politics, and the Bipartisan Campaign Reform Act* (Lanham, MD: Rowman and Littlefield, 2006), p. 42.

31. Jerrold E. Schneider, *Campaign Finance Reform and the Future of the Democratic Party* (New York: Routledge, 2002), p. 28.

32. Matthew J. Burbank, Ronald J. Hrebenar, and Robert C. Benedict, Jr., *Political Parties, Interest Groups and Political Campaigns* (Boulder, CO: Westview, 1999), p. 160.

33. Brian J. Brox, *The New Search for Campaign Effects: Candidates, Parties, and Effects on Voters.* Paper presented at the annual meeting of the Midwestern Political Science Association. Chicago, 2005.

34. James T. Kitchens and Larry Powell, "A Critical Analysis of NCPAC's Strategies in Key 1980 Races: A Third Party Negative Campaign," *Southern Speech Communication Journal,* 51 (1986): 208–28.

35. Jim Drinkard, "Let the Fundraising Begin—Again," *USA Today* (March 10, 2000), 14A.

36. Kate Phillips. "Group Reaches Settlement with F.E.C. over 2004 Campaign Advertising," *New York Times* (March 1, 2007), A16.

37. Jack Hitt, "Campaign Cash," *New York Times Magazine* (July 25, 1999), 20.

38. Wayne, "A Spotlight on Bundling."

39. *Nixon v. Carver,* U.S. District Court 518, U.S. 1033, Springfield, MO, 1996.

40. Wayne, "A Spotlight on Bundling."

41. David Schultz, "States and Campaign Finance Reform," *National Civic Review,* 91, no. 2 (2002): 205–10; Paul Ryan, "Beyond BCRA: Cutting-Edge Campaign

Finance Reform at the Local Government Level," *National Civic Review*, 92, no 1 (2003): 3–18; La Raja, *Small Change*.

42. Richard Braunstein, "Campaign Finance Reform in the American States: The Impact of Contribution Limits on Citizen Behavior and Constitutional Rights," *Spectrum: Journal of State Government*, 75, no. 1 (2002): 38; Donald A. Gross, Robert K. Goidel, and Todd G. Shields, "State Campaign Finance Regulations and Electoral Competition," *American Politics Research*, 30, no. 2 (2002): 143–65.

43. John F. Bibby, "State Party Organizations: Coping and Adapting to Candidate-Centered Politics and Nationalization," in Louis Sandy Maisel (ed.), *The Parties Respond* (Boulder: Westview, 1998), pp. 41–46.

44. Drinkard, "Let the Fundraising Begin."

45. Diane Roberts, *Dream State: Eight Generations of Swamp Lawyers, Conquistadors, Confederate Daughters, Banana Republics and Other Florida Wildlife* (New York: Simon & Schuster, 2004), p. 222.

46. Malcolm E. Jewell and Sarah M. Morehouse, *Political Parties and Elections in American States* (Washington, DC: Congressional Quarterly Press, 2001), p. 64.

47. Clifford J. Levy, "Led by Pataki, Fund Raising in Governor's Race Outstrips the Past," *New York Times* (February 15, 1998), A1.

48. Brian J. Brox, "State Parties in the 2000 Senate Elections," *Social Science Quarterly*, 85, no. 1 (2004): 107–20.

49. James T. Kitchens, e-mail to the author (Dec. 2009).

50. Danny Hakim, "Spitzer's Campaign Finance Reform Stalls over G.O.P. Resistance in Senate," *New York Times* (April 24, 2007), C16.

# 3

# NCPAC and the Development of Third-Party Expenditures

*Larry Powell*

The political activities of 527s in modern political campaigns are not really news. Their history goes back to the 1980s and the formation of Political Action Committees (PACs). Most of those early PACs were devoted to raising money that could be donated to campaigns, but some took advantage of their status to engage in 'independent' third-party campaigns.

The most active and successful of those groups in the early 1980s was the National Conservative Political Action Committee (NCPAC). NCPAC's role in campaigns established an early model of third party expenditures, triggered controversies about the ethical roles of such groups, and eventually triggered a model for campaign responses that are still used by current campaigns.

NCPAC and its chief Terry Dolan burst onto the scene in 1980, using third-party negative ads to trigger upset defeats of several liberal Democrats in the U.S. Senate—Frank Church, George McGovern, and Birch Bayh. They used the same formula (often the same ads, with the names of the candidates changed) in each of their initial campaigns. Their approach relied heavily on direct mail and broadcast ads, with the direct mail campaign serving as both a means of raising funds and also distributing negative information about Democratic incumbents.

NCPAC became the role model for circumventing the campaign reform laws of the day. Those regulations prevented third-party entities from spending more than $1,000 in support of a federal candidate. However, there was no limitation placed on expenditures *against a candidate*. Thus NCPAC geared up to run negative campaigns against those candidates on their "hit list," leaving their candidates to run positive campaigns while separating themselves from the source of the negative ads.

NCPAC's success led the Democratic Party to alter their traditional approach to handling incumbent campaigns and to develop aggressive and anti-negative ads that identified NCPAC as the source of the ad while delineating the tactics used. Those problems eventually led to changes in FEC regulations and the demise of NCPAC as a viable political campaign group.

Still, NCPAC's actions became a model for future groups. NCPAC and the New Right developed a series of third-party strategies that provided the model for those used by current 527 groups. The most obvious aspects of this model were the use of third-party expenditures and negative campaign messages. Those features, and others, continue to be used by 527 groups today.

## NCPAC IN 1980

In 1980, the "New Right" became a major player in the American political scene.[1] The keystone of their campaign was the "Target '80" program aimed at defeating six incumbent Democratic senators—Birch Bayh (Indiana), Alan Cranston (California), Thomas Eagleton (Missouri), Frank Church (Idaho), John Culver (Iowa), and George McGovern (South Dakota). Four of those candidates—Bayh, Church, Culver, and McGovern—were defeated after heavy negative campaigns financed by the New Right. Most of that campaign activity came in the form of independent expenditures by the New Right—expenditures that were independent of the candidate's official campaign structure.

While there are numerous New Right Groups—such as the Moral Majority, the American Security Council, and the Eagle Forum—the National Conservative Political Action Committee (NCPAC) served as the fulcrum for the political campaign activities of the New Right.[2] This group provided the technical expertise for the political activities of the New Right. Although they were not officially and legally part of the challengers' campaigns, many observers concluded that NCPAC had a major influence on the outcome of those elections. Wilbanks, for example, argued that the New Right represented a re-definition of American conservatism.[3] Boydston and Kaid even conducted an experimental study that supported the effectiveness of NCPAC's advertisements.[4]

Other scholars examined the New Right, looking for explanations for their campaign successes. Duffy defined the success in terms of its values.[5] Robinson, Goodman and Price noted how group used different message strategies for different audiences.[6] Bannon argued that the success of NCPAC's strategies were largely a result of timing, for example, developing a strategy that would disrupt the timing of the incumbent's campaign.[7]

One comprehensive analysis of NCPAC's strategies was provided by Kitchens and Powell.[8] That study analyzed NCPAC's campaigns from a three-fold perspective, looking at the campaigns from the perspective of CAT—Contingency, Assumptions, and Techniques.[9]

## Contingent Conditions

Although Richard Viguerie founded NCPAC in 1975, the conditions necessary for success were absent until 1980. To be effective in the 1980 elections, the organization needed a political climate that was conducive to the vulnerability of incumbents, an effective fundraising method, and an efficient grassroots organization to help run the campaign in particular areas. The effectiveness of the New Right was partly a result of these contingencies coming together shortly before the 1980 campaigns.

*Incumbent Vulnerability.* Three factors related to incumbent vulnerability were important to the success of the NCPAC campaigns. First, although the organization supported a broad conservative ideology, it did not identify totally with either the Republican or the Democratic Party. Their approached depended on getting voters to vote against individual incumbents rather than supporting a particularly party. Thus, the group's success depended somewhat on a weakening of voters' allegiances to political parties. That situation did occur. A study of partisan identification from 1952 through 1978 indicated that fewer voters were identifying with either of the two major political parties.[10] This drop in partisan allegiance was crucial since the New Right lacked the credibility that came with being associated with an established party.

Second, since most of the targeted incumbents were Democrats, the New Right needed a political environment that worked against Democratic candidates. That also happened. A study by Democratic campaign consultants following the 1980 election noted a steady decline in votes for Democratic candidates for Congress from 1972 to 1980, especially in the South and West.[11] Thus the political environment was favorable for the defeat of incumbent Democrats, who were the focus of NCPAC's efforts.

Third, the vulnerability of individual incumbents was crucial. NCPAC used benchmark polls to assess individual vulnerability. The scope of this effort is reflected in the midyear budget period, when $1 million was targeted for the use of these polls.[12] As NCPAC leader Terry Dolan said, the group assessed the climate for a conservative candidacy "based on relevant polling data which showed the incumbent weak."[13] For example, George McGovern's defeat was initiated when Arthur Finkelstein, NCPAC's pollster, and Terry Dolan used the polls to convince Republican Congressman James Abdnor to run against McGovern.[14]

*Fundraising.* Although money is an essential element of political campaigns, NCPAC did not have a traditional mechanism for raising campaign contributions in that it lacked a political "personality" who could appeal for financial support. This gap was filled by Richard Viguerie and his affiliated companies by focusing on issues as a basis for raising money. The New Right started this approach in 1970 while raising money for single-issue campaigns.[15] The transition to campaign financing was relatively easy. Viguerie used 15 years of direct mail experience to build a computer list of several million people who responded positively to right-wing appeals.[16]

Opponents of the New Right criticized the cost effectiveness of Viguerie's approach. Out of $2.6 million raised in 1976, for example, only $368,862 was contributed to candidates.[17] Similarly, in 1980, Viguerie spent 79 cents in administrative and mailing costs for every dollar he raised.[18] NCPAC director Terry Dolan responded to the criticisms by saying, "it was meant to be this way. We didn't raise it for candidates, we planned most of it to go to research lobbying, surveys, and other activities to build the conservative base."[19] Thus, direct contributions to campaigns were minimal.

Regardless, Viguerie's fundraising campaign was instrumental in providing New Right groups with financial resources. That included about $2 million per year that went to NCPAC, and $19 million to spend in the 1980 campaigns.[20] Included in its fundraising success were 1979 and 1980 numbers that totaled $7,648,540 for NCPAC.[21]

*Grassroots Organization.* A third condition needed for the New Right's attempt to influence the 1980 elections was an efficient grassroots organization. In the pre-Internet world of campaigns, volunteer labor was needed for mailings, door-to-door canvassing, and for telephone contact with voters. The emergence of conservative religious groups with political goals (e.g., the Moral Majority, the Religious Roundtable) helped fill this gap. By linking themselves to such groups, NCPAC had a direct connection to a grassroots organization that provided millions of potential voters.[22] Their channel of communication was the church, using techniques previously used by Martin Luther King, but putting them to work for conservative causes decades before the idea was developed by Karl Rove and George W. Bush. Not only were local fundamentalist churches a target, but NCPAC understood the influence of the "electronic church." Viguerie noted that fundamentalists could be influential for the New Right because the television clergy had a large and loyal following that could be translated into votes.[23]

Hadden and Swann noted that NCPAC made efforts at recruiting television evangelists for some time before finally succeeding. Such success was vital, the leaders of the New Right thought, because "When you lock horns in social conflict, it's good to have God on your side."[24] Thus the television evangelists could legitimize NCPAC's cause and mobilize the constituencies. NCPAC's biggest success in this effort was gaining the support of Jerry

Falwell and encouraging him to create the Moral Majority. Falwell acknowledged the recruitment while downplaying its intent, saying that Viguerie and Paul Weyrich asked him to lead the Moral Majority, but added, "There is no conspiracy. I don't think I've had more than a couple of meetings with those guys."[25] Regardless, the Moral Majority provided NCPAC with a mechanism for mobilizing grassroots support.

Once the link was established, the organizational process was relatively simple. Televised religious services, radio programs, and "I Love America" rallies helped build a mailing list. That list, plus the enrolling of local ministers for support, provided the primary organization.[26] That primary organization was supplemented with area-wide (city and county) organizational meetings, where local pastors played an important role.[27] In Mississippi, for example, the result was a grassroots organization of "the no-longer silent majority . . . [who] want to know whom to blame and what to do about it."[28] In Illinois, three regional "America, You're Too Young to Die" rallies anchored the organizational meeting, with local ministers coordinating the activities.[29]

Paul Weyrich, the head of the Committee for the Survival of a Free Congress, brought an appreciation of and commitment to grassroots organization for the New Right. Weyrich advocated the "Kasten Plan," an approach which set specific voter turnout goals for every precinct in a congressional district, with a precinct chairman given the responsibility of meeting that goal.[30] Activities included door-to-door visits and telephone contacts with voters identified as supporters of NCPAC's candidates.

Other New Right groups, operating with NCPAC support, organized local religious leaders to guide the political effort. In the organizational plan for Illinois, for example, county organizational meetings were planned for all 102 counties with the goal to recruit 500 pastors and 50,000 other volunteers.[31] Each volunteer received specific goals as part of the larger effort. Although many campaigns use a similar organizational approach, NCPAC was confident of both its ability to organize effectively and of the conservative electorate's response to their effort. Their optimism was based on a belief that such voters had not been effectively organized for earlier elections.[32] As George Zarris, chairman of the Moral Majority of Illinois, said, "We have needed a communication system among the Moral Majority for decades. Now we will have it."[33] Similarly Falwell expected that "there will be several million voting . . . who have seldom voted."[34] Falwell turned out to be overly optimistic, but he did succeed in developing a mailing list of 865,000 voters for the Moral Majority.[35]

Falwell claimed the Moral Majority could deliver four million voters to the cause,[36] but this assertion did not consider regional differences. The Illinois organization produced 40,000 signed anti-ERA ballots within four weeks,[37] but the Tennessee organization generated little enthusiasm and was "undramatic."[38] Regardless, in areas where the organization was successful, NCPAC gained the ground troops for its door-to-door campaigns while providing mail lists for targeted messages. That approach played an important role in a 1982 Senate campaign; political columnists Evans and Novak credited Falwell and the Moral Majority with turning "the tide of Paul Trible's surprise election to the Senate" in an open seat in Virginia by using its organizational list for a late mass mailing.[39]

## Assumptions That Shaped the Messages

The NCPAC strategy identified its target as the politically passive voter who could be reached with negative emotional appeals. Since Dolan apparently assumed an uninformed and low-involved audience that would be highly receptive to a negative campaign, the campaign's message were aimed at a voter who met Nimmo's description of the reactive voter, for example, "a passive machine moved primarily by forces stimulating latent dispositions."[40] For such individuals, voting becomes a decision stimulated by an emotional attachment to symbols. Shadegg described such voters as "those who don't vote at all, or vote only in response to an emotional appeal or as the result of some carefully planned campaign technique which makes it easy for them to reach a decision."[41] To reach such voters, NCPAC considered articulation of specific issues as an essential element. As Viguerie noted:

> They're not really interested in politics. . . . They are interested in the Panama Canal not being given away, reduction of their taxes, a strong national defense, cutting waste and abuse in government programs. That's how people get involved in politics.[42]

That position was supported by research of the time. Specifically, attitudinal research during the 1970s supported the contention that extremity of position is an effective approach with such audiences[43] and using negative appeals made the information more believable.[44]

## Assumptions about Incumbent Behavior

NCPAC also made a crucial assumption about the campaign behavior of the incumbent: as third-party attacks were launched against the incumbent, she/he would ignore the attacks—the classic incumbent response. This response to negative campaigning was described by Murray Chotiner in his early discussions of campaign strategy. Chotiner noted: "When your candidate is under attack . . ., don't answer until the opposition has exhausted its ammunition; you may find the public is disinterested."[45] Chotiner added that the incumbent should respond to an attack only "if you find the attack has reached such proportions that it can no longer be avoided." Then the incumbent should respond "with an attack of your own against the opposition for having launched [their attack] in the first place."[46]

This response works effectively only in situations where challengers are unknown, under-financed, and lack organization. In the campaign of the New Right, adequate financing provided extensive exposure of the message to the public, decreasing the likelihood of finding the public disinterested. NCPAC sought to create an offensive campaign so that NCPAC's issues dominated the campaign agenda while the opposition was "on the defensive," responding to attacks rather than discussing issues that they considered favorable. As one commentator noted, the New Right strategy taught that "if you can sneak up on [an incumbent], [and] if you can set the campaign agenda with a blast of negative advertising and thus put him on the defensive, you've got a chance to beat him."[47] The goal became an attribute-attitude link, or as Dolan noted, "We're hoping the negative will stick, although they [the voters] may not remember why they are so upset."[48]

Usually the incumbent maintains dialogue control by ignoring the attacks and continuing to campaign on issues defined by the incumbent. By ignoring the attack, the incumbent intends to decrease interest in it as an issue. This strategy can be effective if the challenger cannot generate interest in the attack, but it is ineffective if the challenger has sufficient resources to present it to the voters repeatedly. NCPAC's heavy repetition of the ads made it impossible to avoid the attacks as campaign issues.[49] By the time the incumbent responded with the second stage of the classic incumbent response (attack the attack), his/her defense was weakened. If the issued achieved legitimacy, the incumbent's counter attack on NCPAC for launching the attack was viewed as avoiding the issues raised by the negative messages. Both George McGovern and Frank Church, for example, took the classic incumbent response, complaining about NCPAC's campaign but not directly responding to the attacks.[50]

## CAMPAIGN TACTICS

*Vulnerability Assessment.* Ideological shifts increased the number of vulnerable incumbents, but NCPAC still did not attempt a wholesale replacement of senators or congressmen whom they found objectionable. The incumbent had to be evaluated as independently vulnerable. Dolan said the information used to target campaigns was "past voting statistics and all the polling information we can get our hands on."[51]

To provide this data, NCPAC relied heavily on mid-year polls of issues and voter attitudes. This approach contrasted with typical strategies of incumbents at the time. In the 1970s and early 1980s, congressmen rarely used mid-year polls to assess their standing with the electorate, relying instead on internal surveys until the election neared.[52] Those surveys, conducted through Congressional newsletters, were often imprecise both in sample selection and data analysis. In essence, NCPAC's polls were a form of audience analysis that gave them the ability to assess voters' perceptions of acceptable and unacceptable positions on issues. These polls sought both to determine issues that could be used against the incumbent and to evaluate the public's perception of potential opponents.

Much of NCPAC's efforts and financial resources in non-election years was spent in building records of votes which could be used to provide negative information about the targeted incumbents. The Conservative Caucus, concentrating on national issues, produced a "raft of literature on the voting records of individual legislators and 'fact sheets' on controversial issues."[53] For NCPAC, the voting records were both the justification for the attack and the source of material for the negative campaign. As Paul Weyrich said, "There's no question about it. We are a negative organization that wants to get rid of five bad votes in the Senate."[54]

*Third-Party Attacks.* Nine to eighteen months prior to the election, a new committee or local committee of one of the right-wing groups was formed to begin attacking the incumbent.[55] The purpose of these attacks was to hurt the image of the incumbent without the challenger being seen as a mudslinger. Dolan labeled NCPAC's role as doing the "dirty work" of tearing down the credibility of the targeted candidates. This process, he said, "would enable all their challengers to concentrate on image-building without having to wallow in the same muck."[56] Thus NCPAC allowed Republican candidates the luxury of taking the 'high road.' There was no need for mudslinging. . . . NCPAC did it for them."[57] For example, Republican Congressman Steven Symms, who was running against Idaho's Frank Church, said he had "no reason to be interested in a dirty campaign" against Church.[58] And Dolan added, "Steven Symms will never have to say anything about Frank Church. We'll talk about all the negative stuff."[59] For Church, the "negative stuff" included charges of influence selling, "being weak on defense," and of voting for personal pay raises.[60] One direct mail piece labeled Church as "the radical who singlehanded has presided over the destruction of the FBI and the CIA."[61]

Similar negative ads were used in other states. For example, a South Dakota TV ad pictured a basketball player dribbling a ball with this commentary: "Globetrotter is a great name for a basketball team, but it's a terrible name for a senator. While the energy crisis was brewing, George McGovern was touring Cuba with Fidel Castro."[62] In an Indiana ad, a cleaver sliced a large piece of baloney as an announcer said: "One very big piece of baloney is Birch Bayh telling us he's fighting inflation. Sixty-eight billion dollars. That's how much deficit spending Bayh voted for last year."[63]

Dolan believed the third-party attacks gave NCPAC a major advantage in a negative campaign.

> I'm convinced that you can say almost anything . . . you could, in fact, lie. I think the attention span of the voting population, and the fact that there is no connection between us and any candidate makes that perfectly possible and makes this whole thing open to incredible abuse.[64]

Because the attacks came from a third party, Dolan believed that their accuracy was less important. "A group like ours could lie through their teeth and the candidate it helps stays clean," he said elsewhere.[65] Not surprisingly, NCPAC did exactly that. A NCPAC ad aimed at Birch Bayh accused him of voting for an amendment to cut the 1979 defense budget by $1.4 million when Bayh had actually been absent for that vote.[66] Similarly, an ad aimed at Church showed an empty Titan missile silo in Idaho, saying the silo was empty because of Church's opposition to a strong national defense; actually, the silos were empty because the Air Force had replaced the obsolete Titan system with Minutemen missiles Another anti-Church ad incorrectly criticized him for a non-existent vote in favor of a Congressional pay raise.[67]

Another reason for using the third-party attacks was financial in nature. Under the campaign laws of the time, NCPAC was an independent group and thus not limited in financial expenditures. In 1976, the Supreme Court ruled that independent groups could spend unlimited monies on political causes as long as they did not coordinate their activities with any candidate.[68] In contrast, direct contributions to a candidate were limited to $5,000. In essence, the New Right could spend any sum to defeat an incumbent as long as they remained in the role of an independent third party. This ruling led critics to refer to the FEC rulings permitting such expenditures as "Free speech for the rich."[69] In addition, the New Right could easily circumvent the law by having one New Right group, such as the Committee for a Conservative Congress, give direct aid and advice to the challenger, while NCPAC ran the negative campaign independently, a technique that the group itself acknowledged.[70]

To be effective, however, the source of the independent expenditure needed credibility. To avoid any "outsider" image, Dolan suggested finding someone in the state or district to sponsor the negative campaign.[71] By using local members of New Right groups to front the attacks, NCPAC could participate in the electoral process without becoming involved with the structure of either party.

Despite the negative nature of NCPAC's campaign, its approach was distinctively different from that of current 527 groups. NCPAC did not encourage its candidates to take an extreme right-wing position. Quite the contrary, after winning their Republican primary nominations, NCPAC planned for its candidates to "move toward the middle in the general election."[72] In fact, NCPAC and its affiliated groups often offered only conditional support of their candidates, thus making it easier for the candidate to adopt a moderate position. Thus, Falwell's support for Trible in the Virginia senate election had a qualification: Trible was not perfect, but his opponent was far worse.[73]

*In-Kind Contributions.* While NCPAC's campaign was largely independent, they still sought to increase the financial resources of candidates they supported. They did this primarily through the use of in-kind contributions. The laws of the day allowed for in-kind contributions that totaled $5,000—the same limit placed on direct contributions. However, loopholes in the law enabled NCPAC to multiply its monetary impact on the campaign. When carefully handled, $5,000 of in-kind contributions could provide $100,000 worth of campaign services.[74] For example, NCPAC could commission a pollster to conduct a survey of the district; with a copy eventually sent to the candidate. The value of the reported contribution would be the price of making a copy of the survey, not NCPAC's actual cost of conducting the research. In James Abnor's campaign against George McGovern, for example, a campaign poll conducted by NCPAC was reported as a $500 in-kind contribution, at a time when the actual costs of such a poll would have been at least $10,000. Thus, while the total contributions from NCPAC to the Abdnor campaign were within the legal limits, NCPAC's actual expenditures on the campaign was more than $112,000.

*Controlling the Dialogue.* The goal of the New Right approach was to control the dialogue of the campaign. As the campaign began, NCPAC would define the negative issues of the campaign through its third-party ads. The candidate might not immediately attack the incumbent, but—within a few months of the election—he would begin using the same attacks and thus maintain a consistent message. The objective was to have the campaign decided on the bases of issues that had been defined and cast in NCPAC terms. To do that, repetition of the ads and the message was essential. In Idaho, one NCPAC statewide radio spot attacking Church ran 150 times a day for five weeks.[75] Thus George McGovern talked about how NCPAC had cast him as the "anti-family" candidate prior to his return to South Dakota to begin his campaign.[76] Similarly, the "empty silos" representing a weak defense became a major issue in the Church campaign.[77] Such repetitive attacks were often effective at gaining control of the campaign dialogue. As Bannon noted:

> One of the most disruptive aspects of the NCPAC attacks was the havoc they wreaked on Democratic campaign strategy. Many of the Democrats facing re-election in 1980 sought to avoid the impact of the issues such as national defense, government spending, and abortion by basing their campaigns on

their personal qualifications and their long years of public service to their state during their tenure in the U.S. Senate. But the NCPAC attacks changed the campaign agenda, prompting many of the target candidates to abandon their original campaign strategy and respond directly to attacks on their voting records. The candidates put themselves on the defensive, fighting the unconventional battle with unfamiliar weapons.[78]

## DISTINGUISHING CHARACTERISTICS

Although many of NCPAC's tactics were familiar, their campaigns had several distinguishing features. Perhaps its most distinctive feature was its assumption about the response of the incumbent. In other campaign strategies, a classic incumbent response is considered an advantage because the incumbent maintains control of the agenda. But NCPAC's approach used the incumbent's early silence to help them gain control of the campaign agenda.

Closely related to this concept was NCPAC's approach to a negative campaign. That started with its emphasis on repetitive negativism. Through the use of large financial resources, NCPAC was able to reiterate their negative ads constantly. Such constant repetition had two advantages. First, it enabled them to have an impact on the campaign agenda, regardless of the classic incumbent response. Second, it could create negative associations toward the oppositions. Significantly, NCPAC did not consider it crucial that the voters dislike the opponent for the reasons they were advertising. Instead, it was only necessary that a stimulus-response, negative association be triggered, even if those associations lacked the direct ties articulated in the message. In using such an approach, NCPAC differed from those negative campaigns that try to seek specific bi-polar images between the opposition and the incumbent.

A third distinguishing feature was the way the strategy used third-party attacks. Other negative campaigns had used either congruity principles[79] or inoculation theory[80] to dilute the counter charge of mudslinging. But NCPAC's approach was based on a disassociation principle, since the third-part attack generated no direct link between the challenger and the negative campaign generated no direct link between the challenger and the negative campaign.

The New Right's view about voter responses to communicative behavior also provided a distinguishing element. In one sense, the assumption that voters are passive and aroused by emotional appeals corresponds to Shadegg's description of indifferent voters. But NCPAC's stereotypical voter was also issue-oriented and could be politically aroused by anchoring the emotional appeal to those specific issues.[81]

## OTHER CONSIDERATIONS

Evaluations of NCPAC's effectiveness in its campaigns must take into consideration the specifics of the campaigns involved. In the 1980 defeats of Bayh, Church, Culver, and McGovern, the four incumbents were already vulnerable—"burdened by the ravages of concurrent inflation and unemployment."[82] NCPAC also had its setbacks, including the failures to defeat Eagleton and Cranston in 1980 and even less success in the 1982 elections.[83] By 1982, Democratic strategists had developed a new collection of tactics to deal with the groups. Add that to a change in the political environment, and the effectiveness of NCPAC gradually diminished. Still, the group had established a role model for future conservative groups to follow. Elements of the campaign strategy could be seen in the 2004 Swift Boat Veterans campaign against John Kerry and in numerous other negative campaigns against incumbents. Similarly, Charles Black, as senior adviser to the John McCain campaign in 2008, referred to NCPAC while discussing possible strategies for McCain's presidential bid.[84]

## IMPLICATIONS FOR CAMPAIGN FINANCE REFORM

The overall impact of NCPAC as an individual organization was relatively limited. The group made a splash with its defeat of three Democratic senate incumbents in 1980. By the 1982 elections, though, Democratic strategists were ready for their attacks. When the attacks came, the incumbents typically responded with three basic approaches: (1) claiming the opposition was running a mudslinging campaign, (2) identifying the opponent has being part of the mudslinging, and (3) raising issues related to the Fairness Doctrine with the broadcast stations running the NCPAC ads. As *Newsweek* noted, the tactics of the group "became counterproductive and controversial."[85] By 1986, in response to a legal challenge regarding NCPAC's attacks on Sen. Daniel Moynihan (D-NY) in his 1982 re-election campaign, a federal court ruled that the group had gone beyond acceptable spending limits for the campaign.[86]

Ultimately, though, the organization's tactics—and the resulting counter tactics from the Democrats—established the model for third-party campaigns in modern elections. NCPAC was careful to maintain an independent relationship with candidates they supported. While their campaigns were subject to charges of mudslinging, the negative nature of their campaign was a direct result of the campaign laws at the time. Specifically, campaigns that used independent expenditures were prohibited from directly expressing support for a candidate, for example, they could not say "Vote for Candidate X" at any point during their communication campaign.

That requirement essentially made it easier to run a negative campaign against the incumbent than a positive campaign for the challenger. Although either approach could be used, if the groups were careful in their wording, the easier (and legally safer) approach was to use a negative campaign. As a result, modern "527 groups" tend to follow the NCPAC model—run negative ads against a candidate they don't support. In the world of independent expenditures, positive campaigns remain a rarity.

Some of the responses of the Democratic counter strategy have also continued in modern campaigns. The 2000 change in the Fairness Doctrine made that legal challenge obsolete,[87] but the FCC continued to use the doctrine as a guideline for evaluating personal attacks.[88] Further, the basic counter attack of "mudslinging" is still used. Further, most candidates attacked by such group try to tie their opponent to the attacks. In the history of political campaign finance reform, it seems that some things don't change.

## NOTES

1. Richard Viguerie, *The New Right: We're Ready to Lead* (Falls Church, VA: Viguerie Company, 1980).
2. James T. Kitchens and Larry Powell, "A Critical Analysis of NCPAC's Strategies in Key 1980 Races: A Third Party Negative Campaign," *Southern Speech Communication Journal,* 51 (1986): 208–28.
3. Charles Wilbanks, *Ronald Reagan and the New Right: A study in Spacious Rhetoric.* Paper presented at the annual meeting of the Southern Speech Communication Association. Orlando, 1983.
4. John Boydston and Lynda Lee Kaid, *An Experimental Study of the Effectiveness of NCPAC Political Advertisements.* Paper presented at the annual meeting of the Southern Speech Communication Association. Orlando, 1983.
5. Bernard K. Duffy, *The Anti-Humanist Rhetoric of the New Religious Right.* Paper presented at the annual meeting of the Speech Communication Association. Washington, DC, 1983.
6. William L. Robinson, William L. Goodman, and James J. H. Price, *The Rhetoric of the Moral Majority.* Program presented at the annual meeting of the Speech Communication Association. Washington, DC, 1983.
7. Brad Bannon, "NCPAC's Role in the 1980 Senate Elections," *Campaign & Elections,* 3 (1982): 43–46.
8. Kitchens and Powell, "A Critical Analysis."
9. Larry Powell and James T. Kitchens, "Analyzing Campaign Strategies: Contingencies, Assumptions, and Techniques," *Southeastern Political Review,* 14 (Fall, 1986): 161–79.
10. Barbara Hinckley, *Congressional Elections* (Washington, DC: Congressional Quarterly Press, 1981).
11. Gerry S. Tyson, *Congressional Voting Trends: An Examination of Partisan Trends in Congress, 1972–1980* (Fort Worth, TX: Parmer Marketing Company, 1981).

12. Victor S. Kamber and Steven A. Rabin, "PAC Counsel," *Campaigns & Elections*, 2 (1982): 60.
13. Terry Dolan, "Working Today for a Conservative Tomorrow," *Political Action Report*, 2 (1979): 1–4.
14. Maggie Lawson, "McGovern Challenges NCPAC," *Roll* Call (May, 1980): 1.
15. Alan Crawford, *Thunder on the Right* (New York: Pantheon, 1980).
16. Viguerie, *The New Right.*
17. *Federal Election Commission Reports* (1978, March 20).
18. Robert O. Shaw, "'New Right' Only Gives 6 Cents on the Dollar," *Clarion Ledger/Jackson Daily News* (March 29, 1981): 14A.
19. Quoted by William Claiborne, "Little in New Right War Chest Finding Its Way to Candidates," *Washington Post* (March 20, 1978): A1.
20. Shaw, "New Right."
21. *Federal Election Commission Summary*, C 00075390.
22. Jeffrey K. Hadden, and Charles E. Swann, *Prime Time Preachers: The Rising Power of Televangelism* (Reading, MA: Addison-Wesley, 1981).
23. Sid Moody, "The Electronic Church: Spreading the Message," *Clarion Ledger/Jackson Daily News* (October 25, 1981): 1G.
24. Hadden and Swann, *Prime Time Preachers*, p. 142.
25. Quoted by Moody, "The Electronic Church," p. 1G.
26. Hadden and Swann, *Prime Time Preachers.*
27. Michael Clark, "Soldiers of a Christian Right March to Rescue a Backsliding America," *Commercial Appeal* (September 7, 1980): 1A.
28. Michael Clark, "Right's Regiments Unleashed against 'Satanic' Foe," *Commercial Appeal* (September 13, 1980): 1A.
29. "America, You're Too Young to Die," *Moral Majority Report of Illinois* (June–July, 1980): 3.
30. Viguerie, *The New Right*, p. 58.
31. "Moral Majority Fights ERA in Illinois," *Moral Majority Report of Illinois* (June–July, 1980): 3.
32. Viguerie, *The New Right.*
33. "Moral Majority Fights ERA in Illinois," p. 3.
34. Michael Clark, "Early '70s Issue Sent Farwell 'Walking Point'," *Commercial Appeal* (September 10, 1980): 1A.
35. Moody, "The Electronic Church."
36. Hadden and Swann, *Prime Time Preachers.*
37. "Moral Majority Fights ERA in Illinois," p. 3.
38. Clark, "Rights Regiments Unleashed."
39. Rowland Evans and Robert Novak, "Election: What Happened," *Clarion-Ledger* (November 8, 1982): 11A.
40. Dan Nimmo, *Political Communication and Public Opinion in America* (Santa Monica, CA: Goodyear, 1978), p. 364.
41. Steven C. Shadegg, *The New How to Win an Election* (New York: Taplinger, 1972): p. 21.
42. Quoted by James Ridgeway, "The Men Who Stuff Your Mailbox," *Parade* (June 20, 1982): 15–16.

43. Peter Warr and Paul Jackson, "The Importance of Extremity," *Journal of Personality and Social Psychology* 32, (1975): 278–82.
44. Bert H. Hodges, "Effects of Valence on Relative Weighting in Impression Formation," *Journal of Personality and Social Psychology, 30* (1974): 378–81.
45. Quoted by William Costello, "The Facts about Nixon," *New Republic* (October 12, 1959): 11
46. Quoted by Costello, "The Facts about Nixon," p. 12.
47. Don Campbell, "Election's Loser Was the New Right," *Clarion Ledger* (November 8, 1982): 1A.
48. Quoted by Kitchens and Powell, "A Critical Analysis," p. 225.
49. Bannon, "NCPAC's Role in the 1980 Senate Elections."
50. Lawson, "McGovern Challenges NCPAC."
51. Dolan, "Working Today," p. 1.
52. James T. Kitchens, *CIP: Constituent Information Program* (Fort Worth, TX: Parmer Marketing, 1981).
53. "New Right Takes Aim," *Time* (August 2, 1979): 20–21.
54. Quoted by Bernard Weinraub, "Million-Dollar Drive Aims to Oust 5 Liberal Senators," *New York Times* (March 24, 1980): 4.
55. Kitchens, *CIP*.
56. Quoted in "NCPAC's Negative Campaign," *Political Action Report, 5* (1979): 1.
57. Bannon, "NCPAC's Role in the 1980 Senate Elections," p. 44.
58. Quoted in "New Right Takes Aim," p. 21.
59. Quoted in "New Right Takes Aim," p. 21.
60. Bernard Weinraub, "Oust Church Drive in Idaho Stirs Smear Tactics," *New York Times* (May 11, 1980): 20.
61. Quoted in "New Right Takes Aim," p. 21.
62. Weinraub, "Million-Dollar Drive," p. 4.
63. Weinraub, "Million-Dollar Drive," p. 4.
64. Quoted in "NCPAC's negative campaign," p. 3.
65. Quoted by Myra McPherson, "The New Right Brigade," *Washington Post* (August 10, 1980): F1.
66. Bannon, "NCPAC's Role in the 1980 Senate Elections."
67. Weinraub, "Oust Church Drive in Idaho."
68. *Buckley v. Valeo*, 424 U. S. 1, Re: Federal Election Campaign Act of 1971, as amended 1974, 1976, and 1979. 11 C. F. R. 109 (1976).
69. Frank Askin, "Free Speech for the Rich," *Nation*, 251, no. 20 (December 10, 1990): 728.
70. "NCPAC's Negative Campaign."
71. "NCPAC's Negative Campaign."
72. Dolan, "Working Today," p. 4.
73. Evans and Novak, "Election: What Happened."
74. Kitchens and Powell, "A Critical Analysis of NCPAC's Strategies."
75. "New Right Takes Aim."
76. Weinraub, "Million-Dollar Drive," p. 4.
77. Weinraub, "Oust Church Drive in Idaho."
78. Bannon, "NCPAC's Role in the 1980 Senate Elections," p. 44.

79. James T. Kitchens and Betsy Stiteler, "Challenge to the 'Rule of Minimum Effect': A Case Study of the In Man-Out Man Strategy," *Southern Speech Communication Journal*, 44 (1979): 176-90.
80. Larry Powell, "Strategies in a Statewide Secondary Executive Race: A Case Study," *Georgia Speech Communication Journal*, 6 (1977): 19–30.
81. Shadegg, *The New How to Win an Election*.
82. Bannon, "NCPAC's Role in the 1980 Senate Elections," p. 44.
83. Campbell, "Election's Loser."
84. Frank Thomas, "Charlie Black's Cronies," *Wall Street Journal* (July 2, 2008): A11.
85. "Dolan, Leader of the New Right, Dies at 36," *Newsweek*, 109, no. 2 (January 12, 1987): 23
86. "Striking Back at Nick-Pack," *New York Times* (June 1, 1986): A24.
87. J. Robert Craig and B. R. Smith, "The Political Editorializing Rules, the Courts, and Election Year 2000," *Communications & the Law*, 23, no. 3 (2001): 1–17.
88. Robert W. Leweke, "Rules without a Home: FCC Enforcement of the Personal Attack and Political Editorial Rules," *Communication Law & Policy*, 6, no. 4 (2001): 557–76.

## BIBLIOGRAPHY

"America, You're Too Young to Die," *Moral Majority Report of Illinois* (June–July, 1980): 3.

*Buckley v. Valeo*, 424 U.S. 1, Re: Federal Election Campaign Act of 1971, as amended 1974, 1976, and 1979. 11 C. F. R. 109 (1976).

Craig, J. Robert and B. R. Smith. "The Political Editorializing Rules, the Courts, and Election Year 2000," *Communications & the Law*, 23, no. 3 (2001): 1–17.

Hodges, Bert H. "Effects of Valence on Relative Weighting in Impression Formation." *Journal of Personality and Social Psychology*, 30 (1974): 378–81.

Kitchens, James T. and Betsy Stiteler. "Challenge to the 'Rule of Minimum Effect': A Case Study of the In Man-Out Man Strategy." *Southern Speech Communication Journal*, 44 (1979): 176–90.

Nimmo, Dan. *Political Communication and Public Opinion in America* (Santa Monica, CA: Goodyear, 1978).

Powell, Larry and James T. Kitchens. "Analyzing Campaign Strategies: Contingencies, Assumptions, and Techniques." *Southeastern Political Review*, 14 (Fall, 1986): 161–79.

Tyson, Gerry S. *Congressional Voting Trends: An Examination of Partisan Trends in Congress, 1972–1980* (Fort Worth, TX: Parmer Marketing Company, 1981).

Viguerie, Richard. *The New Right: We're Ready to Lead* (Falls Church, VA: Viguerie Company, 1980).

Weinraub, Bernard. "Oust Church Drive in Idaho Stirs Smear Tactics." *New York Times* (May 11, 1980): 20.

# 4

# A History of 527 Organizations

*Melissa M. Smith*

On August 5, 2004, a one-minute political ad from an independent group hit the airwaves in three states and introduced Americans to a new term: 527 organizations. Media coverage of the Swift Boat Veterans for Truth television ads questioning Sen. John Kerry's bravery and service in Vietnam helped the phrase "527 organization" become a household term, even though most Americans were not familiar with the organizations or the rules governing their activities. Coverage by the media often gave the impression that this was a new type of political group, but 527 organizations have actually been in existence since 1975, when Section 527 of the IRS code was added to clarify when campaigns, party committees, and political action committees are exempt from federal income taxes.[1] The groups, which have in the past primarily been organized for non-federal elections, merely moved from the political fringes to a role in the media spotlight during 2004.

The 527s most visible during the 2004 election fell into the current category of groups that were political organizations according to the tax laws, but were not regulated by federal campaign finance laws.[2] Most Section 527 organizations only disclosed the names and addresses of individuals who contributed more than $200 or who received $500 or more from the organization, and the groups were not subject to any contribution limits.[3] In the eyes of many political operatives, these groups presented the best opportunity for distributing political messages without a high degree of government regulation.

Despite how they may have been portrayed in the media, 527s were not new to the political scene in 2004. What *was* different is the influence that these groups had on the campaigns of Senator John Kerry and President George W. Bush and on the American public. The question to be addressed is: How did the 527 organizations, which in the past were mainly utilized to influence state races and referenda, become such an important part of the presidential campaign in 2004? That question will be addressed through the lens of political campaign reform, which has traveled a long and winding road through the American legislative and court systems, and which inadvertently spawned the newly powerful 527 organizations. Those who believe that politics and money make for boring stories should reconsider: Politicians in the United States have a rich history of circumventing existing laws and ignoring those which aren't enforced. The sheer amount of money that is invested in modern campaigns makes this an important subject for review and analysis.

## IMMEDIATE BACKGROUND

Throughout the history of campaign finance reform, three main areas have consistently been the target of regulation: contributions, expenditures, and advertising. Over the years Congress has instituted limits on how much individuals or organizations may contribute to federal campaign committees and political groups, how much campaign committees may spend during the course of an election, and how much money might be used for advertising expenses during a campaign. While the amounts and regulations have changed over the years, the basic idea has remained the same: Try to keep a fairly even playing field for candidates running for federal office and safeguard the political process. Of course, opinions on the effectiveness of these regulations are varied.

The most recent attempt at campaign reform, the Bipartisan Campaign Reform Act (BCRA) of 2002, is also an attempt to regulate contributions, along with what has been termed "issue advertising," or ads which do not expressly advocate a particular candidate, but which can be highly critical or negative. BCRA outlawed "soft money," or large unregulated contributions to political parties[4] and was an attempt to put back into law some reforms first placed on the books in the 1970s. It also sought to re-establish the regulatory framework put into motion by the Federal Election Campaign Act of 1971 and its following amendments.[5] Those regulations (which will be discussed in more depth later) required full disclosure of campaign donations and expenditures, established limits for personal contributions, and charged the Federal Election Commission (FEC) with oversight of political committees. While it sought to restore some of those reforms from the 1970s, one of the main purposes of BCRA was to stem the tide of soft money flooding into campaigns which was used for issue advertising.

Because of new limits set by the BCRA regarding soft money, and because of the FEC's reluctance to regulate these groups, Section 527 organizations simply became the destination for funds which could no longer be donated to national parties, thereby contributing to their strong presence in the 2004 election.

## Why 527s?

To understand the allure of 527 organizations, consider this example: In 2000, actress Jane Fonda donated $11.7 million a few weeks before the presidential election.[6] By splitting her money into two checks over two weeks and donating the money to Pro Choice Vote, a 527 organization which was not required to report the donation to the Federal Election Commission, Fonda was able to avoid drawing attention to her donation from the FEC and the media. Pro Choice Vote then re-distributed Fonda's money to three other pro-choice groups.[7] Although this happened before the passage of the Bipartisan Campaign Reform Act, it is easy to see that the 527 organizations had already become attractive to high-dollar donors. Donors such as Fonda have been able to give large amounts of unregulated money to these organizations, hence the $23.7 million donated by George Soros to 527s during the 2004 campaign, and the $61.8 million donated to and spent by Republican 527s on broadcast advertising during the 2004 election.[8] Although individual contribution amounts above $200 are now reported to the IRS[9] the donation amounts are still not limited by the FEC. Therefore, even after passage of BCRA, Fonda's contribution would be reported, but there would be no limit on how much she might choose to contribute to any particular 527 organization. This makes the organizations quite attractive for large donors who are now unable—because of BCRA—to make large contributions directly to a candidate's campaign or national political party.

In 2004, there were fifty-three groups which focused most of their activity on the presidential election, and these fifty-three groups received $246 million during the 2003–2004 campaign cycle.[10] Of that amount, $146 million came from only twenty-five individuals.[11] It's obvious that there was no shortage of money changing hands during the presidential campaign, but the money wasn't going to the sources where it had mainly been donated in the past: national parties and candidate committees. The reason is that BCRA changed the rules, and so the candidates and their supporters changed their strategies.

To understand why it was originated and the impact that BCRA had on the 2004 presidential campaign, it is necessary to take a stroll through the past to see how campaign finance reform evolved during the 20th and the early part of the 21st centuries. Understanding the path which has been laid in the past gives context to the issues surrounding 527 groups. This is a synopsis of the history of campaign reform—not an exhaustive recitation of all the rules, changes, nuances, and court cases involved in these regulations. In deference to brevity—and sanity, as it is a complicated tale—certain legislation will be considered more in-depth than others.

## EARLY ATTEMPTS AT CAMPAIGN REFORM

Political campaign reform is not a new topic in American politics. Although some elected officials might want Americans to believe otherwise, campaign reform did not originate in the 1990s. In fact, regulations on campaign contributions began in 1867 when Congress made it illegal for any government employee to require workers in naval yards to make political contributions.[12] In 1905, President Theodore Roosevelt attempted to ban all corporate political contributions. This came after Roosevelt was accused of taking campaign gifts from corporations that were interested in buying influence with the administration.[13] Roosevelt denied the accusation, which was later found to have some merit, and called for campaign reform in 1905.[14] In 1907 Roosevelt even argued for the public financing of federal campaigns. However, Congress ignored the idea of public financing and instead passed the Tillman Act, which contained a ban on corporate and national bank contributions to federal campaigns that was easily circumvented.[15]

In 1910 and 1911, Congress set the course for future campaign reform by instituting the first spending limits for federal campaigns and increasing the amount of financial disclosure required by candidates for Senate and House seats.[16] The first successful attempt at extensive campaign reform was the Federal Corrupt Practices Act of 1925, which revised previous campaign reform legislation regarding expenditure limits and disclosure. The Act of 1925 established ceilings on expenditures for candidates running for federal offices, allowing Senate candidates to spend $25,000 and House candidates to spend up to $5,000.[17] However, these limits were applied to party committees, and candidates quickly found a way of getting around this limitation by establishing multiple committees.[18] With power of enforcement vested in Congress, the Act was routinely ignored. In fact, not a single candidate for the U.S. Senate or House of Representatives was ever prosecuted for violating the Act.[19] This Act remained in effect until 1972, when the Federal Election Campaign Act (FECA) became law.

## MAJOR REFORMS IN THE 1970s

Although some additional laws were passed in the intervening years, including the Taft-Hartley Act of 1947 which instituted a permanent ban on labor union contributions to federal election campaigns, the next serious attempts at campaign reform did not materialize until the 1970s, when Congress passed several measures aimed at curtailing the amount of money spent on federal elections. Part of the reasoning behind the new rules in the 1970s was the ever-escalating cost of campaigning. The advent of television had caused a corresponding rise in campaign spending, and many elected officials were concerned about being able to raise the money necessary for upcoming elections.[20] Consider that when he won the presidency in 1860, Abraham Lincoln spent only $100,000 on his entire campaign.[21] However, by 1968, total campaign spending for all candidates had increased to $300 million.[22] Media costs alone increased by almost 600 percent from the 1956 elections to the 1968 contest.[23] This was a cause for concern among many members of Congress, and they set out to change the federal campaign laws.

The first phase of those changes came with the passage of the Federal Election Campaign Act (FECA) in 1971 and its subsequent amendments. FECA replaced the 1925 legislation and required more stringent disclosure requirements for federal candidates, political parties and political action committees (PACs).[24] The 1971 legislation imposed ceilings for media expenditures and required complete disclosure of campaign expenses and disbursements.[25]

FECA required that candidates give a more detailed account than ever before of monies taken in and spent during the campaign.[26] In essence, it was a warm-up for the next thirty years, when campaign reform would be a recurring topic of debate in both Congress and the federal courts, and when future legislation would create loopholes allowing 527s to become important players in federal elections.

The Watergate scandal prompted further amendments and changes in election laws during the 1970s. Although the FECA Amendments of 1974 are seen as additions to the 1971 laws, "this legislation stands as the most comprehensive reform of the campaign finance system ever adopted."[27] In this legislation, Congress set limits on contributions by individuals, political parties, and PACs and strengthened the disclosure provisions of the earlier FECA Act.

## *BUCKLEY V. VALEO*

Congress made two more amendments to the FECA before the end of the '70s. The first was in response to the federal court case of *Buckley v. Valeo* in 1976.[28] Hardly any mention of contemporary campaign reform will be made without referencing this case. In fact, some see the ruling in this case—which lower courts struggled to interpret and apply—as having been one of the biggest obstacles to true campaign finance reform, as they charge it opened the door for unregulated donations to federal campaigns.

Immediately following the passage of amendments to FECA in 1974, a wide-ranging group of plaintiffs, including Sen. James Buckley (R-NY) and liberal activist Stewart Mott, challenged the Act as violating the First and Fifth Amendments. These appeals presented a constitutional challenge to the key provisions of the Federal Election Campaign Act of 1971 as amended in 1974. In its ruling in this case, the Supreme Court found some amendments to FECA to be unconstitutional. In particular, the court found that the limits that had been placed on expenditures by individuals or groups for a specific candidate, on overall campaign expenditures, and on those by an individual candidate from personal funds were unconstitutional.[29]

The contribution limits, however, were upheld by the court. Although the court upheld the limits that had been placed on political contributions by individuals, groups or PACs, it effectively removed the ceiling on what could be *spent* by those running for federal office. The majority opinion stated that limits on what could be spent by individuals, groups or candidates "place substantial and direct restrictions on the ability of candidates, citizens, and associations to engage in protected political expression."[30]

This ruling is widely seen as opening the door for so-called soft money by establishing that political ads not sponsored by a candidate and which do not expressly endorse a particular candidate are not subject to contribution limits or disclosure requirements.[31] This led to a substantial increase in the number of PACs and 527 organizations sponsoring "issue ads" in later elections.

Critics assailed the court's ruling, saying that it equated money with speech, thereby making campaign reform much more difficult to achieve.[32] They argued that removing contribution limits for a candidate's private funds and overall campaign expenditures opens the door for greater abuse of the system by the wealthy and privileged. They also said that the so-called magic word test which came out of the Buckley case—whether or not an issue ad contains words such as "vote for," "vote against," "elect," or "defeat"—was too narrow to be effectively applied and violated the promise of political equality.[33]

In some ways, the 2002 BCRA legislation was an outgrowth of what were seen as the inadequacies of this ruling, as the legislation sought specifically to close the door on soft money and issue ads which had been left open by the Supreme Court.

## SECTION 527 OF THE IRS CODE

Another change which took place in the 1970s which was vital to the development of 527 organizations was the amending of the IRS Code. In 1974 Section 527 of the IRS Code was added to outline when political organizations can be granted tax-exempt status.[34] Prior to this change, political organizations could accumulate investment income that was not reported to the IRS, and some organizations were using this money for the personal benefit of candidates.[35] Under the new IRS rules, political organization income which was labeled as exempt from federal income taxes included: 1) a contribution of money or other property, 2) membership dues or fees, 3) proceeds from political fundraising or entertainment events, and 4) proceeds from conducting bingo games which are used by a political organization.[36] While this did not encourage massive bingo fundraisers by presidential candidates, it did make most of the money collected by political groups (other than net investment income) exempt from the burden of taxes. This was a boon to political organizations, which were defined by the IRS as a "party, committee, association, fund or other organization (whether or not incorporated) organized and operated primarily for the purpose of directly or indirectly accepting contributions for making expenditures, or both."[37] This meant that most money collected was free from taxes, and there were fewer regulations regarding financial disclosure. Groups qualifying for this designation—so-called Section 527 organizations—were required to report their expenditures to the FEC or state agencies, and there were no special requirements that information also be disclosed to the IRS, other than a yearly tax return.[38]

A change occurred in 1996 which encouraged the explosion of 527 organizations in the next five election cycles. The IRS ruled that an "issue advocacy organization that was not registered as a candidate committee, party committee, or PAC" could qualify as a political organization under Section 527 if the primary purpose was to "influence elections," thus granting the organizations tax-exempt status.[39] This meant that an organization did not have to register with the FEC in order to receive the tax-free status. This led to the existence of organizations that were not registered with the government as political committees, but which were able to raise and spend money without being subject to taxation. This very broad definition led to the establishment of many different groups under the Section 527 ruling which were given an almost free hand in fundraising and electioneering.

## REFORM IN THE 1990s

After the IRS ruling in 1996 prompted the sudden growth of Section 527 organizations, these groups began making use of the exception for issue advertising. In the 1996 election, these candidate-specific issue ads began to appear, courtesy of several different 527 groups. "Because a number of federal courts had ruled that communications that did not include terms of express advocacy—such as 'vote for,' 'elect,' or 'defeat,'—were not subject to the restrictions of FECA, party committees and other political groups began to craft broadcast advertisements that featured specific federal candidates but did not include the words that triggered federal regulation."[40] For instance, labor unions decided to use this approach in the 1996 campaign, spending $20 million on issue-type ads mainly aimed at freshmen Republicans.[41] The U.S. Chamber of Commerce also got into the act, spending $7 million to air television ads in 33 congressional districts.[42] Political Action Committees (PACS) funded issue ads, but were not required to disclose who was actually paying for the broadcast messages, thereby leaving some voters confused about who was sponsoring the political messages.

Major political parties also took advantage of this unregulated form of campaigning. In 1996, each party was allowed to spend $12 million supporting its presidential nominee, but by using issue ads, the parties were able to circumvent that requirement without penalties. Each party spent more than $20 million on issue ads.[43]

The trend continued in 2000, when interest groups spent $49 million on issue ads during the election which mentioned specific candidates. These types of advertisements—which were not technically attack ads, but felt like attacks to those in the line of fire—caught the attention of many in Congress and sparked a renewal of campaign reform discussion.

To address what were viewed as the inadequacies of the current campaign laws, a bipartisan coalition was formed in 1996 to address soft money contributions and campaign spending.[44] Legislation favored by Sen. John McCain (R-AZ) and Russell Feingold (D-WI) sought to ban soft money and to make it illegal to use issue advocacy ads in the sixty days prior to an election. The proposed legislation, which had a companion bill presented in the House by Rep. Christopher Shays (R-CT) and Rep. Martin Meehan (D-MA), was debated, tweaked, and modified several times before finally passing both houses of Congress in March 2002. The new law bans most unregulated soft money and places new regulations on the use of issue ads.

## A CLOSER LOOK AT BCRA

After the passage of BCRA in both the House and Senate, President George W. Bush signed the bill despite his own concerns that parts of it might be constitutionally questionable.[45] The ink was hardly dry before supporters and opponents were lining up arguments for federal courts and the FEC. Meanwhile, those planning to run for office in 2004 had to contend with new rules and regulations—many of which made 527 organizations seem the natural way to funnel money into mass communication efforts on behalf of candidates.

The BCRA and its provisions are quite lengthy and detailed, so the main points will be summarized here:[46]

1) *Under BCRA, national political parties are no longer able to collect soft money.* While this may appear to stem the tide of large, unregulated donations to parties, the legislation doesn't cover state parties, which may still collect unregulated political money and then distribute it on behalf of federal candidates.[47] State parties are free to accept so-called Levin funds—

named for Democratic Rep. Carl Levin of Michigan, who suggested this compromise. Under this new category, state and local parties can collect donations as high as $10,000 from corporations, labor unions, and individuals.[48] The money must be used for voter registration and get-out-the-vote activities during federal elections. There is no limit on how much of this can be collected, but the amounts will be reported to the FEC.[49]

2) *The limits on amounts that can be contributed by individuals to candidates running for president, the House and the Senate were raised to $2,000 per election*—from a previous $1,000 limit—and the aggregate limit on annual contributions was raised to $37,500. [50]

3) *The BCRA distinguished a new form of campaign advertising called "electioneering communication."* Under the legislation, an advertisement could qualify as electioneering if it, a) airs thirty days before a primary election or 60 days before a general election, b) refers to a specific candidate for federal office, or c) is targeted to the relevant electorate.[51] The BCRA prohibits electioneering communication, meaning that it prohibits incorporated interest groups from using unregulated money to pay for broadcast advertising that uses the likeness or name of a candidate within these 30- or 60-day time periods. This does not cover other types of media, such as print advertising or direct mail.[52]

This restriction extends to non-profit corporations and incorporated political committees as defined by Section 527 of the IRS code. Later FEC action exempted non-profit charities, which are already prohibited from political activity under the tax laws. The restriction does not apply to organizations that are not registered as political committees, which exempts many 527 groups.

## SECTION 527 GROUPS IN THE 2004 ELECTION

The proliferation of 527 organizations in the 2004 election campaign was not totally unexpected. As early as fall 2002, some political watchers and journalists were predicting a rise in the number of independent political groups. "The [BCRA] barely regulates independent organizations like labor unions, trade associations, 527s like Pro Choice vote, and issue-oriented groups like the Sierra Club and the National Rifle Association. These groups are all free to expand without limits. Already, fundraising by 527s is exploding, with the fifty most active of them raising nearly $11 million in just the first three months of 2002."[53] Even before the bulk of the 527 ads began appearing, there was rising concern about how the flow of unregulated money was going to be diverted. Political watchdog groups in late 2003 asked the FEC to take a tougher regulatory stance with 527s. "If 527s aren't stopped now, the Republicans will be sure to catch on to them by the next election and use them better than Democrats ever hoped to, since it's no new revelation that the Republican Party has more deep-pocketed supporters than the Democrats."[54] Calls for the FEC to enforce its rule requiring any 527 group which is attempting to affect a federal election to register as a federal political committee—and therefore only be able to use hard money—were unsuccessful, and the 527s worked free of most regulation during the 2004 campaign.[55]

### Big donors, Big Impact

Because they were relatively free of federal regulation, the 527 organizations raised and spent more than a half-billion dollars between 2003 and 2004, which is double the amount that these types of organizations spent in the 2002 election cycle.[56] Take for example the Progress for America Voter Fund, a 527 group, which reported raising almost $45 million and spending $35.4 million during the campaign. This 527 was not listed among the top money-raising 527 organizations in either the 2000 or the 2003 election cycle. The same can be said for MoveOn.org Voter Fund and the Swift Boat Vets and POWs for Truth, both of which spent more than $20 million in the 2004 election.[57]

Individuals who made substantial contributions to 527s during the 2004 election cycle included George and Susan Soros, who gave $23.7 million; Peter B. Lewis, who contributed $23.3 million; Stephen L. Bing, who gave $13.7 million; and Herb and Marion Sandler, who contributed $13 million.[58] From these amounts it is easy to see that during the 2004 election Section 527 organizations became the destination for funds that previously would have gone to national parties or PACs, both of which were limited by BCRA.

Another reason that so many new 527 organizations appeared in the 2004 election cycle is the relative simplicity of the organizations: ". . . it only takes a few individuals willing to part with millions of dollars to fund groups like ACT and Progress for America. These groups can surge onto the scene in the future. We saw a proliferation of 527 organizations this year, and we'll see them again next cycle."[59] In fact, eight of every ten dollars taken in by 527s supporting Kerry came from donors who gave $250,000 or more.[60] Such 527 organizations are generally smaller and more flexible than a campaign committee, and usually don't have the same layers of infrastructure and organization seen in state and national parties. However, they are often run by political professionals, and frequently rely on the same resources as a political campaign, including polls, focus groups and media consultants.[61]

Did BCRA cause a decrease in the amount spent on advertising in the 2004 campaign? The answer is a definite "no." In fact, total spending on political advertising and related marketing surged past previous records, reaching $2.74 billion for the full year in 2004.[62] Total political spending increased 126.1 percent when compared with the numbers from the 2000 presidential campaign.[63] Bush and Kerry raised more than any previous presidential candidates, but, because of BCRA restrictions, they were required to spend all of it before the national conventions. The legislation required that money not spent prior to national conventions to be donated to the respective national parties. "The key driving overall growth in 2004 was the dramatic increase in campaign donations at both the national and local levels, especially by the Democratic Party candidates and 527 groups that resulted in levels equaling the Republicans."[64] The largest share of political spending on media came in the presidential race, which garnered 37.8 percent of the overall media spending. That compares with 25.3 percent in 2000.[65]

The Nielsen Monitor-Plus and the Wisconsin Advertising Project, a political research group run by the University of Wisconsin's political science department, analyzed the campaigns and advertisements from both campaign committees and independent organizations and found that ads produced by 527 groups were predominately negative. In fact, the group found that independent groups aired "no purely positive spots" between September 24 and October 7, 2004.[66] Project researchers also found that candidate ads tended to be more positive than messages produced by political parties and independent groups. This finding was echoed by a content analysis of television ads from the campaign which found that 81 percent of the independent group ads analyzed were negative, compared to only 50 percent of the candidate-sponsored ads.[67]

According to several analyses of the 2004 advertising messages, it seems that candidates allowed the 527 groups to broadcast the most negative messages, thus avoiding the possible boomerang effect that negative advertising can sometimes cause.[68] The lax regulation of these groups probably worked to each candidate's advantage, as the independent organizations—some of which had strong ties to individuals involved in presidential campaigns—produced hard-hitting ads which were aimed at undercutting the opponent's credibility. "The Swift Boat Veterans attack was masterful. This group delivered a message that the Bush campaign and the RNC could not, and Bush got the best of both worlds because he could decry the 527s and benefit from their activities at the same time."[69] Likewise, Kerry benefited from the 527s, as his campaign produced mostly contrast ads, while the Kerry-supporting 527s crafted negative messages aimed at Bush.

This brings up an important question: Did the BCRA reduce the effect of soft money on the election process? It does not seem to have slowed the amount of money flowing into the campaigns, as the amount of money spent on all races in 2004 topped $4 billion. "Clearly, McCain-Feingold did nothing to reduce the influence of money and perhaps made things worse. By Oct. 1, presidential candidates had spent over $340 million, $100 million more than was spent in the entire 2000 year cycle."[70] The Democratic National Committee, sensing what was about the happen, launched a secret initiative to divert soft money to 527s even as BCRA was being debated on the Senate floor.[71] "We would laugh bitterly when we saw Democratic senators on the floor saying, 'Let's get big money out of politics and go back to grass-roots politics.'"[72]

Even one of the sponsors of the BCRA, Rep. Marty Meehan (D-MA) opined after the election that record amounts of soft money flowed into the 527s during the 2004 election. Meehan said more than $400 million found its way into Section 527 groups to influence the election. "Unfortunately, during an election cycle when grassroots activity flourished, a small set of organizations were allowed to play by a different set of rules. 527 groups became the preferred vehicle for large donors to steer enormous sums of soft money into federal elections."[73] Meehan was one of several legislators to call for tougher regulation of 527s by the FEC.

Those calls for regulation resulted in few changes, and 527 organizations were influential in several states during the 2008 primaries. MoveOn.org published a newspaper attack ad against Gen. David Petraeus ("General Betray Us") that triggered $500,000 donations in one day, which set a record for the organization.[74] Criticism of Sen. John McCain's comment that the U.S. might stay in Iraq for one-hundred years became an issue primarily because 527 groups—particularly those funded by MoveOn.org and the American Federation of State, County and Municipal Employees—spent $500,000 on ads that ran in Michigan, Ohio and Wisconsin and on CNN and MSNBC featuring his comments.[75] Both Obama and McCain benefited from 527s, although those supporting Obama seemed better funded.

## BCRA'S EFFECT ON FUNDRAISING

Two of the reasons given for the necessity of BCRA was to help even the playing field for federal candidates and lessen the impact of unregulated soft money on elections. However, it hasn't had that effect.

In fact, because of the loophole allowing 527s to use unregulated soft funds, there is more money than ever flowing into federal elections. Total spending in the 2004 presidential election—from all sources seeking to influence the race—was more than $1.7 billion. In comparison, the total in 2000 was just under $1 billion. Both Bush and Kerry chose to forgo public funds in their primary campaigns, which increased the total amount in 2004, but there was also an increase in the amount of money donated to political parties and candidates by small individual donations.

That trend continued in the 2008 race, as Sen. Barack Obama broke all previous presidential candidate fundraising records. He was confident enough in his fundraising projections to also reject public financing for the general election, making him the first candidate from a major party to turn down the public funds. A significant percentage of his campaign money came from small personal donations, although Democratic bundlers—individuals who are charged with raising large amounts of cash—were still utilized.

This renewed reliance on small donors might give the impression that BCRA has successfully removed the influence of big donors on presidential campaigns. This is not really true. BCRA actually raised individual contribution amounts, and individuals can also contribute up to $25,000 to a political party each year.[76] While candidates like to play up the amounts coming from small individual donations—that makes them seem much more popular with the public and less beholden to special interests—they are less likely to talk about the amount of money coming to campaign committees through bundlers. By August 2008, the Obama campaign was quick to note the amount that had flowed into the campaign from individuals giving $200 or less.[77] However, at that time Obama also had contributions from 552 bundlers, 15 of whom were lobbyists. His total amount raised at that point was $336,724,305.[78]

Little is also said about how many bundlers are lobbyists or work in particular industries. For instance, as of Sept. 18, 2008, the McCain campaign had 64 people connected to Wall Street who had raised $11.4 million.[79] By that same date, Obama had raised $8.9 million through Wall Street bundlers, making the fall 2008 crisis on Wall Street a somewhat personal issue for the candidates, as much of their money was flowing through that venue.[80]

Political parties, which claimed they would be at a disadvantage because of BCRA, actually broke all fundraising records in 2003–2004. The Democratic National Committee raised $389.8 million, while the Republican National Committee raised $385.3 million, giving the Democrats a fundraising advantage for the first time since the 1970s. Both parties seem to have adapted to the new rules, and both seemed to flourish in the first major national election since BCRA took effect.

While the national parties raised a lot of money, how the money was spent was dictated by BCRA rules. In the 2004 and 2008 races, there appeared to be less coordination between the parties and the federal campaign committees. While national parties in the past have served to provide an umbrella for candidates (working with state parties, developing themes, and promoting party cohesion), federal campaigns are now less of an organized traffic flow than parallel highways. Coordination between 527 organizations and campaign committees or parties is not allowed under BCRA, so at times it seemed there were several different campaigns underway for a single candidate. The candidate's committee was running one campaign, the party was running another, and independent groups were also supporting a candidate through uncoordinated advertising and marketing. Still, as Luo noted, "the candidates, while often distancing themselves from these efforts, certainly benefit from their activities."[81]

While some might argue that this gives independent groups an advantage over political parties, it has actually benefited the parties in two ways. First, national parties have been forced to broaden their donor bases. Instead of relying on large donations of soft money, as had previously fueled much of the parties' coffers, the national organizations have shifted to a reliance on smaller donations. This has worked to the parties' advantage, as the organizations have returned to grass-roots supporters and developed donor lists that will help both candidates and the parties in the future. This was one of the ways in which national parties had to evolve after BCRA, and it seems to be working. In the 2008 race, the parties broke the fundraising records set in 2004, as both Republicans and Democrats had already raised more than $400 million by summer 2008.

The 527 groups, meanwhile, played an active role in the 2008 election—starting in January. Wayne noted that the ads filled "a void before the February 5 primaries, as campaigns run short of money."[82] In the New Hampshire Republican primary, an abortion-rights group ran television ads attacking Mitt Romney for his changed position on abortion.[83] A group called "The Club for Growth" spent $700,000 attacking Mike Huckabee's record on taxes while he was governor of Arkansas.[84] Barack Obama distanced himself from a California group, Vote Hope, but the group continued to work on his behalf in the state.[85] Meanwhile, another group (The American Leadership Project) ran ads in Pennsylvania on behalf of Hillary Clinton.[86] By April 2008, the 527 groups became particularly important to the Clinton campaign, which was running short on cash. With many of her donors "maxed out" to her and the party, some of those donors started giving money to the 527s as a way to help her campaign.[87]

Once the nominees were certain, both Democrat Barack Obama and Republican John McCain requested that the 527s stay out of the campaign. MoveOn.org, which had sponsored ads attacking McCain in the primaries agreed to stay out and actually dismantled its 527 group.[88] On the Republican side, Freedom Watch—which had planned to oppose MoveOn.org—found itself limited by financial and organizational problems.[89] Republican groups, in particular, were facing a shortage of funds. As Luo noted, "Many wealthy donors who might be in a position to finance a 527 group . . . or a similar independent effort that is free to accept unlimited contributions are wary this time because of the legal problems that dogged many such groups after the 2004 election."[90]

The legal problems in question were typified by the "Swift Boat Veterans" group from the 2004 election. A group of veterans who supported John Kerry had challenged the ads, taking up an offer by billionaire Boone Pickens to pay a million dollars to anyone who could refute any single point made in the ads.[91] The Kerry supporters identified ten mistakes in the Swift Boat ads but, when presented with the challenge, Pickens backed off of his offer.[92] That didn't end the problems for the Swift Boat veterans or other Republican-backed 527s. The FEC ruled that the Swift Boat Veterans had illegally spent $20 million in 2004; they were fined $299,500, while another 527—Progress for America—was fined $750,000.[93] The legal rulings were enough to temper donor enthusiasm for the groups. Still, that didn't stop the activities of the 527s. Billionaire Harold Simmons, a McCain supporter, donated $2.9 million to a group that ran ads about Obama's association with former black radical William Ayers.[94] Other groups sponsored ads linking Obama and his former pastor, Rev. Jeremiah Wright.[95]

## STATE AND NATIONAL PARTIES

While money may have been flowing into the 527 and independent groups' coffers, state and national parties have been looking for alternate ways to raise cash. BCRA didn't just bring about changes in the national parties. State parties were also forced to make changes in how they are funded. Because they once relied on money from national parties that usually came from soft donations, state parties have also been forced to adopt a funding model that increases reliance on small donors and gives them greater potential grassroots support. Observers argue that this can have positive or negative effects on state parties, as it causes them to rely on more grassroots support within their states. That might work well for the predominant party in a state, but it could cause shortfalls in states without a strong minority party.

Another change for national parties is that they now have the option of spending unlimited amounts of money during an election, as long as they do not coordinate with a candidate's campaign committee. They also are able to make coordinated expenditures that are subject to federal limits. While this may seem to undermine the role of the party in federal elections, it is more of an evolution, rather than a devolution. Over the years, while the influence of the two major American political parties has waxed and waned, the overall goal—to institute particular policies in government—has not changed.

Oftentimes the strength of a party is measured through its electoral achievements—how many individuals allied with the party are elected to office — but that is not the full picture. Parties work behind the scenes to develop social capital that will enable them to push through their public agendas. They provide a platform for those with diverse interests to come together to push for change, and in the process they forge links with individual Americans. In this respect, BCRA has had a positive effect on the national parties. They are raising more money than before, and much of it is coming from the grass-roots level, which makes a party more accountable than before.

A new reliance on independent party expenditures by both campaigns and the parties can be seen as having a negative effect on the party. However, this reliance can serve to partially "free up" the party from what was once expected during an election. Independent organizations often run more negative advertisements during an election, thus allowing parties to focus on particular issues, rather than serve in the role of "attack dog" for a federal candidate. Of course, the parties still often produce and air negative advertisements, but the marketing load can now be shared by campaigns, parties, and independent groups.

In the case of John Kerry in 2004, the three uncoordinated campaigns (Kerry's committee, the Democratic Party, and independent groups) produced materials that sent mixed messages and themes to the public. This is one of the potential drawbacks to having uncoordinated messages produced by several different organizations. In that same election, President George W. Bush benefited from independent organizations and party ads that attacked Kerry and generally produced messages with themes echoing those of the Bush campaign. In both cases, 527 groups played a major role in providing information and images to the American public.

This seems like a natural evolution, as American society seems to moving through a change in which individuals are given more control over their ability to make their voices heard. From YouTube to personal blogs to viewer-supplied reports on CNN and FoxNews, Americans are able to share their thoughts and observations with more people than ever before. This is reflected in the trend toward a greater participation (or some would argue reliance) on independent groups in national and state elections. While BCRA has indeed changed the rules regarding who and what can finance political activity, those same rules have worked to push parties closer to their members and give greater ability for independent voices to be heard in an election.

While there may be some positives to come out of BCRA, the overall goals of the reform have fallen short. It seems likely that, no matter what type of campaign reform is passed by Congress or the FEC, campaigns and independent groups will look for ways to circumvent those rules. As history has shown, most recently through BCRA, a way will be found (in this case 527 organizations) to continue to pump large sums of money into campaigns, and the parties will not only survive, but learn to thrive in the new environment.

## IS LIMITING CAMPAIGN CONTRIBUTIONS THE WAY TO REFORM?

Beyond BCRA and the influence of Section 527 organizations lies a more fundamental question: Why has there always been such an emphasis on the regulation of political contributions?

According to one commentator, "the distasteful reality is that politics requires money."[96] Reformers reason that greater regulation of campaign funds might allow for a more level playing field for those who are not already in office or who don't have the same financial resources. Plus, limiting contributions seems like a good way to avoid situations in which certain individuals or corporations have great influence over policy and decision making. "Those who defend the constitutionality of campaign finance regulation generally adopt one of more of the following three positions. The first position . . . the looming threat of quid pro quo arrangements between candidates and supporters justifies some sort of regulation. Under this reasoning, contribution limits squarely address the governments interest in preventing the appearance and reality of corruption."[97] The other two approaches involve an effort to "equalize the relative ability of all citizens to affect the outcome of elections" and the justification of finance regulation in the name of political equality.[98] Of these three approaches, the one most often supported by the U.S. Supreme Court and used again in support of the BCRA restrictions—is that of regulation as an attempt to prevent corruption.

But not all attempts at regulating campaign donations have been successful or popular. Alongside those who champion contribution limits are those who say that enforcing such limits is equal to the regulation of political speech, which is discouraged by the First Amendment. Before BCRA, the U.S. Supreme Court had voiced a somewhat mixed review, striking down some legislation dealing with campaign contribution limitations, but upholding others. For instance, in the case of *Buckley v. Valeo* the Supreme Court upheld the campaign disclosure requirements, but struck down limits placed on candidate expenditures (unless those candidates accept public financing for campaigns) and on independent expenditures. The court reasoned that the limitations added up to a breach of free speech rights.

However, in its 2003 decision regarding *McConnell v. Federal Election Commission*—the first challenge to BCRA to make it before the Supreme Court—justices ruled that the wording and application of BCRA is focused "narrowly on those soft-money donations with the greatest potential to corrupt or give rise to the appearance of corruption of federal candidates and officeholders."[99] Thus, the justices upheld the BCRA restriction on issue ads within thirty days of a primary and sixty days of a general election.

The decision in a more recent case, however, seems to indicate that the current court is not as willing to accept some restrictions placed on issue advertising. In *FEC v. Wisconsin Right to Life*, the court ruled 5-4 that an ad may be considered "the functional equivalent of express advocacy" only if it is "susceptible of no reasonable interpretation other than as an appeal to vote for or against a specific candidate." "The test to distinguish constitutionally protected political speech from speech that BCRA may proscribe should provide a safe harbor for those who wish to exercise First Amendment."[100] This ruling was seen by some as an opening for corporations to divert funds to electioneering communications, as the high court ruled that the Wisconsin Right to Life ads, which were paid in part through corporate funds, were deemed "issue advocacy," rather than express advocacy. "The shadings between attacks on candidates' views on the issues and attacks on their character may be difficult to discern. If the FEC tries to enforce BCRA, the corporations and unions will claim that their ads are issue advocacy and assert as-applied challenges to BCRA in their defense."[101]

While some support campaign reform, others, especially those unhappy with the *Buckley v. Valeo* decision in 1976, say that the current situation is one in which true opportunities for democratic government are fading. "Buckley makes it more difficult to create the participatory conditions necessary for self-government by placing a constitutional choke on legislative reforms aimed at equalizing effective access to community deliberation on public issues."[102] In 1997, House Minority Leader Richard Gephardt said that, "What we have is two important values in conflict: freedom of speech and our desire for healthy campaigns in a healthy democracy. You can't have both."[103]

Indeed, that seems to be a belief that is echoed often among those who support campaign reform. Representatives of the National Voting Rights Institute complained that, by removing campaign spending limits, Buckley equated money with free speech. This, they have argued, undermines public confidence in elections and increases the likelihood of corruption and fraud. ". . . the ruling wrongly undermines the principle of political equality by allowing wealthy candidates to stifle the ability for candidates with less money to compete fairly in the electoral arena."[104]

Ideas about how to achieve a more balanced system vary, with communitarians such as Cass Sunstein urging less of an emphasis on individual interests. Sunstein offers the idea that "efforts to redress economic inequalities should not be seen as impermissible redistribution . . . we should evaluate campaign finance laws pragmatically in terms of their consequences for the system of free expression."[105] Others advocate a different approach, saying that a better idea would be to "let candidates raise [money] from as many sources as possible—and to let the public see who's giving. That would be true reform."[106] In other words, this approach would abandon contribution limits, but increase controls on disclosure. Another less supported idea is to forbid candidates from accepting private contributions and publicly fund elections—which sounds similar to what Theodore Roosevelt proposed early in the twentieth century.

The one thing that is certain is that the debate over campaign reform will continue to resurface every few years. So far, the FEC has resisted pressure from Congress that it more tightly regulate the 527s, and many of the changes put into place have been struck down by the courts. If the FEC and the courts continue to resist the calls for greater regulation, it is certain that 527 groups will remain a popular destination for wealthy individuals seeking to influence politics, and they will continue to play a pivotal role in federal elections.

## NOTES

1. The Brookings Institution, "Recent Developments in Campaign Finance Regulation. Section 527 Organizations." (2001), www.brookings.org/gs/cf/headlines/527_intro.htm (20 June 2005). Michael J. Malbin, *Life after Reform. When the Bipartisan Campaign Reform Act . . . Meets Politics* (Lanham, Md.: Rowman & Littlefield, 2003)
2. Brookings, "Recent Developments."
3. Brookings, "Recent Developments."
4. Michael Scherer, "Campaign Finance Reform School," *Columbia Journalism Review* (1 Sept. 2002): 41–44. Malbin, *Life After Reform.*
5. Malbin, *Life After Reform.*
6. Scherer, "Campaign Finance Reform."
7. Scherer, "Campaign Finance Reform."
8. Center for Public Integrity, "527s in 2004 Shatter Previous Records for Political Fundraising." (30 March 2005), http://www.publicintegrity.org/527/report.aspx?aid=435 (20 June 2005).
9. U.S. Code, Title 26, Subtitle A, Chapter 1, Subchapter F, part VI, Section 527.
10. Center for Public Integrity, *527s in 2004*.
11. Committee on House Administration, "Testimony by the Honorable Marty Meehan." (20 April 2005), http://cha.house.gov/hearings/Testimony.aspx?TID=568 (3 Jan. 2006).
12. Center for Responsive Politics, "A Brief History of Money in Politics: Reform Attempts at the Federal Level," www.opensecrets.org/pubs/history/history3.html (1 Jan. 2006).
13. Anthony Corrado, Thomas E. Mann, Daniel Ortiz, Trevor Potter, & Frank J. Sorauf, *Campaign Finance Reform: A Sourcebook* (Washington, D.C.: Brookings Institution Press, 1997).
14. Corrado, *Campaign Finance Reform.*

15. Corrado, *Campaign Finance Reform.*
16. Corrado, *Campaign Finance Reform.*
17. Alexander, "Financing Politics." J.E. Cantor, "Campaign Financing in Federal Elections: A Guide to the Law and Its Operation," in *Campaign Financing in the United States Issues and Laws,* ed. Auguste V. Anschutz (New York: Nova Science Publishers, 2002), 55–105.
18. Alexander, *Financing Politics.* Corrado, *Campaign Finance Reform.*
19. Center for Responsive Politics, A Brief History.
20. Corrado, *Campaign Finance Reform.*
21. Alexander, *Financing Politics.*
22. Alexander, *Financing Politics.*
23. Corrado, *Campaign Finance Reform.*
24. Corrado, *Campaign Finance Reform.* Alexander, *Financing Politics.*
25. Corrado, *Campaign Finance Reform.*
26. Alexander, *Financing Politics.*
27. Corrado, *Campaign Finance Reform,* 53.
28. *Buckley v. Valeo,* 424 U.S. 1.
29. *Buckley v. Valeo,* 424 U.S. 1.
30. *Buckley v. Valeo,* 424 U.S. 1.
31. Ryan Ellis, "Electioneering Communication under the Bipartisan Campaign Reform Act of 2002," *Case Western Reserve Law Review,* no. 54 (2003): 187–224. Cantor, "Campaign Financing."
32. Christopher Banks, & John Green, (1999). "A Symposium: The Legal and Political Implications of Buckley v. Valeo," *Akron Law Review,* 33, no. 1, (1999): 1–106.
33. John C. Bonifaz, Gregory Luke, & Brenda Wright, "Challenging Buckley v. Valeo: A Legal Strategy," *Akron Law Review,* 33, no. 1 (1999): 1–106.
34. Brookings, "Recent Developments."
35. Subcommittee on Oversight of the House Committee on Ways and Means, 2000.
36. U.S. Code, Title 26, Subtitle A, Chapter 1, Subchapter F, part VI, Section 527.
37. U.S. Code, Title 26, Subtitle A, Chapter 1, Subchapter F, part VI, Section 527.
38. Brookings, "Recent Developments."
39. Brookings, "Recent Developments."
40. Malbin, *Life After Reform,* 28.
41. Malbin, *Life After Reform.* Julie Kosterlitz, "Laboring Uphill," *National Journal,* 28, no. 3 (1996): 474.
42. Malbin, *Life After Reform.*
43. Ellis, "Electioneering Communication."
44. Glenda C. Williams, "Pleading the Fifth: Media Economics, Free Air Time and the Fifth Amendment," *Communication Law & Policy,* 6, no. 2 (2001): 319–54.
45. Malbin, *Life After Reform.* Ellis, "Electioneering Communication."
46. Federal Election Commission, "*Reform Act of 2002 (BCRA),*" 2002, search.freefind.com/find.html?x=0&y=0&id=50985594&pageid=r&mode=ALL&n=0&query=BCRA (15 Dec. 2005).

47. Scherer, "Campaign Finance Reform."
48. Malbin, *Life After Reform.*
49. Scherer, "Campaign Finance Reform."
50. Scherer, "Campaign Finance Reform." Malbin, *Life After Reform.*
51. Ellis, "Electioneering Communication." Malbin, *Life After Reform.*
52. Scherer, "Campaign Finance Reform." Malbin, *Life After Reform.* Ellis, "Electioneering Communication."
53. Scherer, "Campaign Finance Reform," 55.
54. Roy Speckhardt, "Are New Campaign Finance Regulations an Attack on Free Speech?" *Humanist,* 64, no. 3 (2004): 6.
55. Alliance for Better Campaigns, *Facts about 527s,* (n.d.), http://www.bettercampaigns.org/freeairtime/factsheets/527s (28 Dec. 2005).
56. Center for Public Integrity, *527s in 2004*
57. Center for Public Integrity, *527s in 2004.*
58. Center for Public Integrity, 527s in 2004. James V. Grimaldi, & Thomas Edsall, Super Rich Step into Political Vacuum. McCain-Feingold Paved Way for 527s,*Washington Post,* 17 Oct. 2004, A01.
59. Center for the Study of Elections and Democracy, "527s Had a Substantial Impact on the Ground and Air Wars in 2004, Will Return," 16 Dec. 2004, http://www.publicintegrity.org/docs/527/pdf2.p (20 June 2005).
60. Grimaldi & Edsall, "Super Rich."
61. Center for Study of Elections and Democracy, "527s Had Substantial."
62. Patrick Quinn & Leo Kivijarv, "US Political Media Buying 2004," *International Journal of Advertising,* 24, no. 1 (2005): 131–40.
63. Quinn & Kivijarv, "US Political Media."
64. Quinn & Kivijarv, "US Political Media," 134.
65. Quinn & Kivijarv, "US Political Media."
66. Wisconsin Advertising Project, *Presidential TV Advertising Battle Narrows to Just ten Battleground States,* (12 Oct. 2004), http://polisci.wisc.edu/tvadvertising (5 Jan. 2006).
67. Lynda Lee Kaid & Daniela Dimitrova, "The Television Advertising Battleground in the 2004 Presidential Election," *Journalism Studies,* 6, no. 2 (2005) 165–75.
68. James King & Jason McConnell, "The Effect of Negative Campaign Advertising on Vote Choice: The Mediating Influence of Gender," *Social Science Quarterly,* 84, no. 4 (2005) 843–57. Amy E. Jasperson & David P. Fan, "An Aggregate Examination of the Backlash Effect in Advertising: The Case of the 1996 Senate Race in Minnesota," *Journal of Advertising* 31, no. 1 (2002) 1–12. Karen Johnson-Cartee, & Gary Copeland, "Southern voters' reaction to negative Political Ads in 1986 Election," *Journalism Quarterly,* 66 no. 4 (1989) 888–986.
69. Center for Study of Elections and Democracy, "527s Had Substantial."
70. Dan Hellinger, "The Party is Over but the Campaign Beat Goes On," *St. Louis Journalism Review,* 34, no. 27 (2004) 26–27.
71. Grimaldi & Edsall, "Super Rich."
72. Grimaldi & Edsall, "Super Rich," A01.
73. Committee on House Administration, "Testimony by."
74. David M. Herszenhorn, "Senate Approves Resolution Denouncing MoveOn.org Ad," *New York Times,* 21 Sept. 2007, A16.

75. Jim Rutenberg, "The ad campaign: Taking on McCain for a Comment on the War," *New York Times*, 19 June 2008, A20.

76. Raymond J. La Raja, *Small Change: Money, Political Parties, and Campaign Finance Reform* (Ann Arbor: University of Michigan Press, 2008).

77. "Obama Camp Reports $66 Million in Donations in August," FoxNews, 14 Sept. 2008, elections.foxnews.com/2008/09/14/obama-camp-reports-66m-in-donations-in-august/ (24 Sept. 2008).

78. "Data Points: Barack Obama's Bundlers," *U.S. News & World Report*, 26 Aug. 2008, www.usnews.com/articles/opinion/2008/08/26/data-points-barack-obamas-bundlers.html (24 Sept. 2008).

79. Foon Rhee, "Wall Street Bundlers Helping Both McCain, Obama," *Boston Globe*, 18 Sept. 2008, www.boston.com/news/politics/politicalintelligence/2008/09/wall_street_bun.html (24 Sept. 2008).

80. Rhee, "Wall Street Bundlers."

81. Michael Luo, "Facing Obama Fund-Raising Juggernaut, Clinton Seeks New Sources of Cash," *New York Times*, 20 April 2008, A20.

82. Leslie Wayne, "Outside Groups Aid Obama, Vocal Critic of Their Influence," *New York Times*, 20 Jan. 2008, A1, A18.

83. Michael Luo, "Romney Attacked Over Abortion," *New York Times*, 3 Dec. 2007, A18

84. Luo, "Romney Attacked."

85. Wayne, "Outside Groups Aid."

86. Michael Luo, "New Support for Clinton," *New York Times*, 16 April 2008, A22.

87. Luo, "Facing Obama."

88. Rutenberg, "The Ad Campaign."

89. Michael Luo, "Great Expectations for a Conservative Group Seem All but Dashed," *New York Times*, 12 April 2008, A13.

90. Michael Luo, "Ready to Attack Obama, if Some Money Arrives," *New York Times*, 21 June 2008, A1, A12.

91. Kate Zernike "Veterans Rebut 'Swift Boat' Charges Against Kerry in Answer to Challenge," *New York Times*, 21 June 2008, A17. Kate Zernike, "Veterans Fight to Reclaim the Name 'Swift Boat,'" *New York Times*, 30 June 2008, A1, 15.

92. Kate Zernike, "Thanks, but no Reward," *New York Times*, 26 June 2008, A16.

93. Leslie Wayne, "Swift Boat Financier Finds Efforts Are Muted," *New York Times*, 26 Oct. 2008, A29.

94. Jim Rutenberg, "A Billionaire Finances Ads Hitting Obama," *New York Times*, 23 Aug. 2008, A12.

95. Jim Rutenberg, "Pinpoint Attacks Focus on Obama," *New York Times*, 24 Sept. 2008, A1, A16.

96. Robert J. Samuelson, "Making Pols into Crooks," *Newsweek*, 1997, no. 14, 53.

97. William J. Connolly, "*How Low Can You Go? State Campaign Contribution Limits and the First Amendment*," 76 B.U.L. Rev. 483 (1996).

98. Connolly, *How Low Can.*

99. Legal Information Institute, *McConnell v. Federal Election Commission* (02-1674) 540 U.S. 93, http://supct.law.cornell.edu/supct/html/02-1674.ZS.html (25 Aug. 2005).

100. *FEC v. Wisconsin Right to Life*, No. 06-969, Bench opinion.

101. Summary of Supreme Court Decision in *FEC v. Wisconsin Right to Life* (2007), Brennan Center for Justice at NYU School of Law. www.brennancenter.org/content/resource/summary_of_supreme_court_decision_in_fec_v_wisconsin_right_to_life_pdf/ (11 Aug. 2008).

102. Jeffrey Abramson & Elizabeth Bussiere, "Free Speech and Free Press. A Communitarian Perspective," *Responsive Community*, 4 no. 2 (1994): 22–32.

103. Steve Chabot, "Campaign Finance and Freedom of Speech. Congressional Testimony," (2001), commdocs.house.gov/committees/judiciary/hju73134.000/hju73134_0f.htm (15 Oct. 2003).

104. Banks & Green, "A Symposium."

105. Cass Sunstein, "Speech in the Welfare State: Free Speech Now," 59 U. Chi. L. Rev. 255 (1992).

106. Samuelson, "Making Pols into Crooks."

## BIBLIOGRAPHY (PARTIAL)

Abramson, Jeffrey and Elizabeth Bussiere. "Free Speech and Free Press. A Communitarian Perspective." *The Responsive Community*, 4 no. 2 (1994): 22–32.

Alexander, Herbert. *Financing politics. Money, Elections, and Political reform* (Washington D.C.: Congressional Quarterly, 1984).

Brookings Institution. "Recent Developments in Campaign Finance Regulation. Section 527 Organizations."(2001) http://www.brookings.org/gs/cf/headlines/527_intro.htm (20 June 2005).

Bonifaz, John C., G.G. Luke, and B. Wright. "Challenging Buckley v. Valeo: A Legal Strategy." *Akron Law Review*, 33, no. 1 (1999): 1–106.

Center for Public Integrity, *527s in 2004 Shatter Previous Records for Political Fundraising*. (30 March 2005) www.publicintegrity.org/527/report.aspx?aid=435 (20 June 2005).

Center for the Study of Elections and Democracy. "527s Had a Substantial Impact on the Ground and Air Wars in 2004, Will Return," 16 Dec. 2004, www.publicintegrity.org/docs/527/pdf2.p (20 June 2005).

Corrado, Anthony, T.E. Mann, D. Ortiz, T. Potter, and F.J. Sorauf, F.J. *Campaign Finance Reform: A Sourcebook* (Washington, D.C.: Brookings Institution Press, 1997).

Grimaldi, James V. and Thomas Edsall, "Super Rich Step into Political Vacuum. McCain-Feingold Paved Way for 527s." *Washington Post*, 17 Oct. 2004, A01.

Luo, Michael. "Ready to Attack Obama, if Some Money Arrives," *New York Times*, 21 June 2008, A1, A12.

Rutenberg, Jim. "Pinpoint Attacks Focus on Obama." *New York Times*, 24 Sept. 2008, A1, A16.

Speckhardt, Roy. "Are New Campaign Finance Regulations an Attack on Free Speech?" *Humanist*, 64, no. 3 (2004): 6.

Summary of Supreme Court Decision in FEC vs. Wisconsin Right to Life (2007), Brennan Center for Justice at NYU School of Law. www.brennancenter.org/

content/resource/summary_of_supreme_court_decision_in_fec_v_wisconsin_right_to_life_pdf (11 Aug. 2008).

Wisconsin Advertising Project. *Presidential TV Advertising Battle Narrows to Just Ten Battleground States,* (12 Oct. 2004), http://polisci.wisc.edu/tvadvertising (5 Jan. 2006).

Zernike, Kate. "Veterans Rebut 'Swift Boat' Charges against Kerry in Answer to Challenge." *New York Times,* 21 June 2008, A17.

# 5

# Swift Boat Veterans vs. MoveOn.org

*Glenda C. Williams*

On August 5, 2004, a small group called Swift Boat Veterans for Truth torpedoed the American voters, and launched a new awareness of the power of independent groups in the political process. Although their ads only originally aired in three states, media coverage of their message quickly spread and became a major part of the political discussion.

On the other side of the political aisle, an established group called MoveOn.org had already launched an anti-Bush campaign, but with little fanfare. The emergence of Swift Boat Veterans, however, quickly brought MoveOn to the forefront of the political battle. Although neither of these groups was endorsed by a candidate, they were able to raise and spend extraordinary amounts of money in the 2004 presidential campaign. While numerous 527s participated in the campaigns, Swift Boat Veterans and MoveOn generated the most attention in the media.

As noted in chapter 5, through the campaigning of these two groups, American voters were introduced to a new term: "527 organizations." Named after their exemption status in the IRS code, the 527s brought a fiercely negative tone to the campaign. This chapter will discuss both Swift Boat Veterans for Truth and MoveOn.org, examining their history and contributions to the 2004 campaigns.

## MOVEON.ORG

MoveOn.org was founded in September 1998 by Joan Blades and Wes Boyd in response to the impeachment controversy surrounding President Clinton.[1] They launched a petition, "Censure President Clinton and Move

On to Pressing Issues Facing the Nation"; hundreds of thousands signed.[2] Energized by the response, Blades and Boyd began to look for ways to involve these grassroots people in the political process. MoveOn.org Civic Action became the involvement arm of the organization, while the Voter Fund was the official 527 for political action funding. Their stated goal was to support progressive candidates who had the best interests of the American people in mind.

In late 2001, MoveOn was joined by Eli Pariser, the founder of MoveOn Peace campaign. Originally formed after 9/11, MoveOn Peace called for restraint in response to the terrorist attacks; shortly after forming this new group, Pariser merged with MoveOn.org and became the executive director.[3]

The MoveOn Voter Fund was greatly utilized during the 2004 campaign.[4] MoveOn reported that the Fund "raised approximately $11 million for eighty-one candidates from over 300,000 donors."[5] Some observers praised the organization for "giving citizens an opportunity to lodge democratic challenges against the state during hostile political climates."[6] The Center for Responsive Politics, however, reported that, in 2004, more than $5 million was given to MoveOn by only two donors: George Soros and Peter Lewis.[7] Another bundle of money came from a series of big-name concerts that included a performance by Bruce Springsteen.[8]

Much of these contributions were channeled into television spots. And as established in chapter 5, the ads were overwhelmingly negative. MoveOn's national ads against George Bush began on April 27 on FOX and CNN; other negative ad campaigns aired only in battleground states throughout the summer and into the fall.[9] The first ads compared the military records of Senator John Kerry and President George Bush. Called "Kerry/Bush," these portrayed Bush in a negative light and Kerry in a positive light. This was the only positive message relayed by MoveOn.

Other negative ads followed, including "Hooded," which called for the resignation of Defense Secretary Donald Rumsfeld; "Platter," about Halliburton and "no-bid" contracts; "Burgers" and "Debate," which both focused on jobs going overseas; "Gay Marriage," which called for a focus on "real problems;" and the "Real People" series, which showcased testimonials from former Bush supporters who were now supporting Kerry.[10] Thousands of dollars went into these ads, all of which hammered George Bush.

In June 2008, almost ten years after its formation, MoveOn.org announced in an email to its members that it was shutting down its 527 Voter Fund and using only its political action committee (PAC) instead.[11] Stating that this move was an "all-in commitment to the small-donor way of doing things," the email asked all its members to contribute in small ways. MSNBC reported that Obama had benefited more from 527s than McCain, but quoted an insider who claimed that the move was designed as a "dare" to Republicans.[12] If the Republicans didn't accept support from 527s, they would hurt themselves financially. If they did accept support from 527s, McCain would look weak.[13]

In 2006, MoveOn reported 3.2 million members. By mid 2008, they reported more than 5 million members and contributions over $122 million for their political action committee (PAC).[14] Today, MoveOn continues to operate as a PAC. Accepting only donations of $5,000 or less, MoveOn allows contributors to designate where the money should go. MoveOn then distributes the money and files the FEC paperwork on behalf of the contributor.

## SWIFT BOAT VETERANS FOR TRUTH

As noted, the "Kerry/Bush" ads, comparing the military service of Senator John Kerry and President George Bush, first aired on April 27, 2004. On May 4, 2004, Swift Boat Veterans for Truth went public at a press conference at the National Press Club in Washington, D.C.[15] These Vietnam vets repudiated the claims regarding Kerry's war record. Organizers of the Swift Boat Veterans included Rear Admiral Roy Hoffman and John E. O'Neill.[16] Funding came from numerous veterans, as well as from businessman Bob Perry, who contributed $200,000 and was listed in the FEC report as the largest contributor.[17] Other reports, however, credited Texas millionaire Sam Fox as the largest contributor.[18]

The first television ad, "Any Questions?" aired in only three states, beginning on August 5, but it ignited a national hailstorm of controversy. The ad claimed that John Kerry lied to receive the medals he was awarded in Vietnam, and refuted his version of what happened in those incidents. The vets featured in the ad had served in Vietnam during John Kerry's time of service, making their testimony strong and persuasive.[19] Talk shows on cable television and on radio stations across the country picked up on the ads and discussed them on-air. Because of this free media exposure, a poll conducted by the Annenberg Public Policy Center (August 9–16) showed that over 57 percent of all Americans had either seen or heard of the ad during the eleven days after the ad launched.[20]

MoveOn.org mobilized a rebuttal, creating its own ad, "Swift Response," demanding, "George Bush: Take that ad off the air" and attacking his military record.[21] The ad debuted on August 17, airing on the same stations the Swift Boat Veterans had used, along with FOX and CNN. The Swift Boat Veterans kept the ads coming, however, challenging Kerry's actions and decorations: "Atrocities," "Why," and "They Served" all used testimonies and appearances from Vietnam vets themselves. But Swift Boat also created several ads using the audio recording of Kerry's appearance before the U.S. Senate's Committee on Foreign Affairs from April 22, 1971. To many political observers, these ads, "Dazed," "Sell Out," and "Medals" seemed to reflect the true reason behind the Swift Boat campaign: during Kerry's appearance before the committee, he had testified to numerous atrocities and war crimes allegedly committed by the majority of U.S. troops serving in Vietnam. The Swift Boat Veterans were, in their own words, still furiously angry over what they dubbed his betrayal. Another spot, "Friends," tied Senator Kerry to Jane Fonda, another anti-Vietnam activist. The public, embroiled in the first show-down between two 527s, actually paid attention. However, most voters lined up along partisan lines.[22]

After two weeks, President Bush did criticize the Swift Boat ads, but not individually—he grouped them with all 527 ads, in many of which he was the primary target. In a statement to the press, he said, "That means that ad, every other ad. I can't be more plain about it. And I wish—I hope my opponent joins me in saying—condemning these activities of the 527s. It's—I think they're bad for the system. That's why I signed the bill, McCain-Feingold."[23]

On August 5, the Kerry campaign released an extensive report on Kerry's military service, but stopped short of releasing his complete military records. On August 25, one of the Swift Boat Veterans' founders released his book on the topic: *Unfit for Command: Swift Boat Veterans Speak Out Against John Kerry* by John E. O'Neill. This book, like the ads, called into question Kerry's service, decorations, and actions. Its primary focus, though, was on Kerry's testimony to the Senate committee, his anti-war demonstrations, and his rejection of his medals. The book sparked as much controversy as the ads, with Vietnam vets lining up on both sides of the argument.

## FINAL ANALYSIS

MoveOn.org and The Swift Boat Veterans for Truth were not the largest 527s, nor did they generate the most money during the 2004 elections. However, their media battle elevated the 527s to an unprecedented level. The word "liar" was attributed to both sides of the battle, but who was telling the truth?

FactCheck.org, a project belonging to the Annenberg Public Policy Center, found that all of the ads from both groups contained twisted or falsified messages. Their in-depth analysis called the Swift Boat ads "dubious," and stated that the MoveOn ads contained "distorted claims."[24] In short, neither group presented a clear, non-partisan position.

The FEC agreed. In December of 2006, the FEC ruled that the "overtly partisan activities" of these two groups "crossed the line."[25] Admonishing that both groups should have organized as official PACs, the FEC fined Swift Boat $299,500; MoveOn was fined $150,000.[26]

In June 2008, MoveOn announced that it was dropping its 527 Voter Fund and establishing the MoveOn PAC. The Web Site for Swift Boats states that "Swift Vets and POW for Truth formally disbanded and ceased all operations on May 31, 2008."[27]

## NOTES

1. MoveOn.org, www.moveon.org/about.html.
2. MoveOn.org, www.moveon.org/about.html.
3. MoveOn.org, www.moveon.org/about.html.
4. Andrew Chadwick, "Digital Network Repertoires and Organizational Hybridity," *Political Communication,* 24, no. 3 (2007): 283–301.
5. MoveOn.org, http://www.moveon.org/about.html.
6. Deana A. Rohlinger and Jordan Brown, "Democracy, Action, and the Internet after 9/11," *American Behavioral Scientist,* 53, no. 1 (2009): 133.
7. OpenSecrets.org.
8. Caroline Zaayer, "They'll be Dancin' in the Dark—at Home," *American Journalism Review,* 26, no. 5 (2004): 23.
9. Center for Responsive Politics, (2009). www.opensecrets.org/527s/527events.php?id=41.
10. Center for Responsive Politics.
11. Eli Pariser, Press Release, 20 June 2008, firstread.msnbc.msn.com/archive/2008/06/20/1158252.aspx (27 Dec. 2009).
12. MSNBC, firstread.msnbc.msn.com/archive/2008/06/20/1158252.aspx (2008).
13. MSNBC, 2008.
14. Pariser, "Press Release."
15. Source Watch, "MoveOn," Center for Media & Democracy, 2009, www.sourcewatch.org/index.php?title=MoveOn.org.
16. Source Watch, MoveOn.
17. Center for Responsive Politics.
18. Source Watch, MoveOn.
19. George N. Dionisopoulos, "Incident on the Bay Hap River and the Guns of August: The Swift Boat Drama and Counter-Narrative in the 2004 Election," *Communication Quarterly, 57,* (2009): 487–511. Jeremy M. Teigen, "Veterans' Party Identification, Candidate Affect, and Vote Choice in the 2004 U.S. Presidential Election," *Armed Forces and Society,* 33, no. 3 (2007): 414–37.
20. Annenberg Public Policy Center, "Cable and Talk Radio Boost Public Awareness of Swift Boat Ad," 20 Aug. 2004, www.annenbergpublicpolicycenter.org/NewsFilter.aspx?mySubType=ALL&.
21. Howard Kurtz, "MoveOn.org's Swift Response to Anti-Kerry Ad," *Washington Post,* 17 Aug. 2004, A8.
22. Annenberg, "Cable and Talk Radio."

23. MSNBC, "Bush Calls for Halt to Swift Boat Veterans' Ads: President Calls So-called 527 Ads 'Bad for the System,'" 23 Aug. 2004, http://www.msnbc.msn.com/id/5797164/.

24. FactCheck.org, "The Whoppers of 2004," Annenberg Political Fact Check, 31 Oct. 2004, http://www.factcheck.org/article298.html.

25. Richard Simon, (2006). "Fec Fines Swift Boat, Moveon: It Says the '527' Groups Crossed the Line With Overtly Partisan 2004 Campaign Activities," *Nation*, 14 Dec. 2006, http://articles.latimes.com/2006/dec/14/nation/na-swift-boat14

26. Simon, "FEC Fines."

27. Swift Boat Veterans for Truth, www.swiftvets.com.

## BIBLIOGRAPHY


Annenberg Public Policy Center. "Cable and Talk Radio Boost Public Awareness of Swift Boat Ad," August 20, 2004. www.annenbergpublicpolicycenter.org/NewsFilter.aspx?mySubType=ALL& (29 December 2009).

Center for Public Integrity. http://www.publicintegrity.org (29 December, 2009).

Center for Responsive Politics. 2008. www.opensecrets.org/527s/527events.php?id=41 (29 December 2009).

Center for the Study of Elections and Democracy, csed.byu.edu/Research/Past%20Projects/Pew2004.dhtml (27 December, 2009).

Chadwick, Andrew. "Digital Network Repertoires and Organizational Hybridity." *Political Communication*, 24, no. 3(2007): 283–301.

Dionisopoulos, George N. "Incident on the Bay Hap River and the Guns of August: The 'Swift Boat Drama' and Counter-Narrative in the 2004 Election." *Communication Quarterly*, 57 (2009): 487–511.

Dobbs, Michael. "Swift Boat Accounts Incomplete: Critics Fail to Disprove Kerry's Version of Vietnam War Episode," August 22, 2004, *Washington Post*, A1.

FactCheck.org. "Would Bush Eliminate Overtime Pay for 8 Million?" Annenberg Political Fact Check, March 5, 2004. www.factcheck.org/elections-2004/would_bush_eliminate_overtime_pay_for_8.html (27 December 2009).

FactCheck.org. "Anti-Bush Ad Overstates Case Against Halliburton," Annenberg Political Fact Check, June 28, 2004. www.factcheck.org/anti-bush_ad_overstates_case_against_halliburton.html (27 December 2009).

FactCheck.org. "Republican-funded Group Attacks Kerry's War Record," Annenberg Political Fact Check, August 22, 2004. www.factcheck.org/article231.html (27 December 2009).

FactCheck.org. "The Whoppers of 2004," Annenberg Political Fact Check, October 31, 2004. www.factcheck.org/article298.html (29 December 2009).

FactCheck.org. "MoveOn.org Social Security Ad," Annenberg Political Fact Check, February 2, 2005. www.factcheck.org/socialsecurity/print_moveonorg_social_security_ad.html (27 December 2009).

FactCheck.org. "Caught 'Red-Handed?'" Annenberg Political Fact Check, April 27, 2006. www.factcheck.org/elections-2006/print_caught_red-handed.html (27 December 2009).

Kurtz, Howard. "MoveOn.org's Swift Response to Anti-Kerry Ad." *Washington Post*, August 17, 2004, A8.

MoveOn.org. www.moveon.org/about.html (28 December 2009).

MSNBC. "Bush Calls For Halt to Swift Boat Veterans' Ads: President Calls So-Called 527 Ads 'Bad for the System.'" August 23, 2004. www.msnbc.msn.com/id/5797164/ (3 January 2010).

O'Neill, John E. *Unfit for Command: Swift Boat Veterans Speak Out Against John Kerry*. (Washington, DC: Regenery Publishing, 2004.)

Pariser, Eli. Press release, June 20, 2008. firstread.msnbc.msn.com/archive/2008/06/20/1158252.aspx (27 December 2009).

Piereson, James. "Senator Kerry & the Swift Boat Vets." *New Criterion*. August 18, 2008. www.newcriterion.com/posts.cfm/Senator-Kerry---the-Swift-Boat-vets-4999 (3 January 2010).

Rassman, Jim. "Shame on the Swift Boat Veterans for Bush: John Kerry Saved My Life. Now His Heroism is Being Questioned." *The Wall Street Journal*, 10 August 2004, A10.

Rohlinger, Deana A., and Jordan Brown. "Democracy, Action, and the Internet after 9/11." *American Behavioral Scientist*, 53, no. 1 (2009) 133–50.

Simon, Richard. "FEC fines Swift Boat, MoveOn: It Says the '527' Groups Crossed the Line with Overtly Partisan 2004 Campaign Activities." *The Nation*, December 14, 2006. articles.latimes.com/2006/dec/14/nation/na-swiftboat14 (29 December 2009).

Source Watch. "Swift Boat Veterans for Truth," Center for Media & Democracy, 2004. www.sourcewatch.org/index.php?title=Swift_Boat_Veterans_for_Truth (3 January 2010).

Source Watch. "MoveOn," Center for Media & Democracy, 2009. www.sourcewatch.org/index.php?title=MoveOn.org (30 December 2009).

Swett, Scott. "Media Still Lying about the Swift Boat Veterans." *American Thinker*, May 25, 2009. www.americanthinker.com/2009/05/media_still_lying_about_the_sw.html (30 December 2009).

Swett, Scott and Tim Ziegler. *To Set The Record Straight: How Swift Boat Veterans, POWs and the New Media Defeated John Kerry*. (Falls Church, VA: New American Media Publishing, 2008).

Swift Boat Veterans for Truth. www.swiftvets.com (30 December 2009).

Teigen, Jeremy M. "Veterans' Party Identification, Candidate Affect, and Vote Choice in the 2004 U.S. Presidential Election." *Armed Forces and Society*, 33, no. 3 (2007) 414–37.

VandeHei, Jim, and Farhi, Paul. "POWs Shown in Film Join Swift Boat Group's Anti-Kerry Efforts." *Washington Post*, October 14, 2004. www.washingtonpost.com/wp-dyn/content/article/2004/10/14/AR2005033105699.html (3 January 2010).

WinterSoldier. "Swift Boat Veterans for Truth," *New American Media Online Services*, May 2004. www.wintersoldier.com/index.php?topic=SwiftVets (29 December 2009).

Zaayer, Caroline. "They'll be Dancin' in the Dark—at Home." *American Journalism Review, 2004, 26(5)*, 23.

Zernike, Kate. "Kerry Pressing Swift Boat Case Long After Loss." *The New York Times*, May 28, 2006, A1.

# 6

# Analysis of 527 Ads in 2004 Election

*Barry P. Smith and Melissa M. Smith*

Every presidential candidate knows going into the race that he or she will have to produce and air television ads. The amount spent on television ads by candidates dwarfs the money spent on other types of advertising media, and that is still holding despite the transformation underway in the media because of the Internet.[1] In 2006, a year in which there was no presidential election, $2.2 billion was spent on political advertising—more than the amount spent on ads during the 2004 presidential election. The majority of that money was spent on local broadcast television, with much smaller amounts going to cable television, radio, newspapers, and the Internet.

The number and style of television ads produced by candidates will vary, but millions of dollars are poured into the making and airing of political advertisements during each election season. Although the Internet has demonstrated its value in presidential campaigns, the use of television ads in political contests has not significantly declined. For instance, in the 2008 campaign, in one week of television advertising—from September 28 through October 4—the Obama campaign spent almost $17.5 million and the McCain campaign spent almost $11 million.[2] Most of that money was spent in battleground states, while some states—those where victory was almost assured by one candidate—were virtually ignored.

Advertising in the 2004 presidential campaign presented a shift in the political landscape, both in terms of the messages sent to voters and in terms of who paid for those messages. This was the first presidential election since the Bipartisan Campaign Reform Act was signed into law, and it was seen as a test of the ability of BCRA to rein in soft money and the influence of independent groups. However, in the 2004 race, President George W. Bush, Sen. John Kerry and various independent groups "spent more money on more advertisements across more media channels than in any previous U.S. election."[3] The significance of independent political groups and their expenditures in the 2004 election cannot be overlooked, as individual donors poured millions into these organizations in an effort to influence the election.

## WHY INDEPENDENT POLITICAL GROUPS?

When the Bipartisan Campaign Reform Act of 2002 (also known as McCain-Feingold) was signed into law, national parties lost the ability to accept large amounts of unregulated money from individuals. In 2000, the national parties raised $487 million from corporations, labor unions and wealthy individuals.[4] Commonly known as "soft money," these large donations had become very important to national parties, as there were basically no regulations on how it must be spent.

After BCRA became law, these organizations and individuals needed another outlet for their political donations. So-called 527 organizations provided that outlet, as they were able to accept unlimited donations and were subject to few regulations by the Federal Election Commission. In the 2004 presidential election, 527 organizations (named for a particular section of the IRS code) became popular conduits for large donations, and they spent almost $150 million to air television commercials in support of or against presidential candidates.[5]

In 2004, there were fifty-three groups which focused most of their activity on the presidential election, and these fifty-three groups received $246 million during the 2003–2004 campaign cycle.[6] Of that amount, $146 million came from only twenty-five individuals.[7] It is obvious that there was no shortage of money changing hands during the presidential campaign, but the money was not going to the sources where it had mainly been donated in the past: national parties and candidate committees. The reason is that BCRA changed the rules, and so the candidates and their supporters changed their strategies.

Take, for example, the Progress for America Voter Fund, a 527 group, which reported raising almost $45 million and spending $35.4 million during the campaign. This 527 was not listed among the top money-raising 527 organizations in either the 2000 or the 2004 election cycle.[8] The same can be said for MoveOn.org Voter Fund and the Swift Boat Vets and POWs for Truth, both of which spent more than $20 million in the 2004 election.[9]

Because rules prevent coordination of messages between political campaigns and other organizations, there are basically three parallel political campaigns (for each candidate) running at once: the candidate's official campaign, the national party campaign, and independent organization campaigns. In 2004 these independent organizations produced and aired television ads in support of or opposing presidential candidates, thus running their own "campaigns" for the candidates. The lack of coordination, however, can backfire for some candidates. Although Bush seems to have benefited from many of the Republican-leaning 527-group ads, Kerry was not helped, and could have been harmed, by the number of mixed messages being broadcast to American voters.[10]

## LOOKING AT THE ADS

Devlin's analysis of the 2004 primary advertisements notes that the Kerry media team produced 42 ads, while Edwards—his closest competitor—produced twenty-three.[11] The majority of his ads were aired in the last three months of the primary, at a cost of about $858,000. Because the Democratic primary was a hard-fought contest, both Kerry and Edwards raised and spent a large percentage of their money on television spots. This outlay of cash (which had to be spent by the Democratic convention in the summer) left Kerry's campaign cash-poor following the Democratic convention.

Swift Boat Veterans for Truth, a 527 group dedicated to portraying Kerry as unfit for command, chose that point to begin airing its ads. The first ad was "Any Questions" and featured 13 Vietnam veterans who said they served with John Kerry. Four of these veterans called Kerry a liar. The 60-second spot was aired in small markets in Ohio, West Virginia, and Wisconsin and set the course for the group's attack ads. The media picked up on the ads, playing portions of them in newscasts, and talk show hosts gave free air time to the group and its messages.[12] The timing of these ads hurt Kerry, as he did not have the resources to respond. In response to Kerry's complaints, Bush called for the group to moderate its attacks, but he benefited greatly from the group's negative ads.

This set the tone for the general election, in which the Republican-leaning independent groups and 527 organizations generally worked to Bush's benefit, but the Democratic-leaning 527s did little to help Kerry. This occurred despite the fact that the Kerry-supporting 527s actually spent almost twice as much money as did those supporting Bush.[13] One analysis of the independent group ads found that the Kerry campaign and the pro-Kerry groups may have diluted their message, and that the timing of the expenditures worked in favor of President Bush.[14] The pro-Kerry groups spent heavily early in the general election, but the pro-Bush groups outspent them 3-1 in the final three weeks of the election.[15]

Early analyses of ads aired during the 2004 presidential election showed that the overwhelming majority of independent group ads were negative.

The pro-Bush independent groups seemed to have a strategy of emphasizing Kerry's character weaknesses in negative ads, while the pro-Kerry groups instead focused more on issues in mostly negative ads.[16] Negative attack messages from independent groups allowed the candidates to air more positive spots and decrease the number of negative ads aired by the campaigns. As noted before, the pro-Bush groups aired messages that were more reinforcing of Bush's selected campaign messages and themes, while those supportive of Kerry often differed significantly from their candidate's campaign in the specific issues addressed in their ads. The result was a clear, reinforced message for Bush, and a lack of clarity and effectiveness for Kerry.

## CONTENT ANALYSIS

Because of the importance of independent group expenditures in the 2004 race, the ads produced by those groups should be examined more carefully. Previous studies have provided insight into the number, tone, and overall impact of the ads, but a more comprehensive look is necessary to help gauge the impact of these ads on the presidential election.

### Sample

To that end, thirty-four campaign ads from the 2004 presidential general election were content analyzed. These ads comprised all the 527-group ads from the collection archived and analyzed by Devlin.[17] Devlin's archive of ads from each presidential campaign cycle have been widely used and recognized as a reliable sample for analysis.

There were four organizations responsible for the production of the ads in our sample. There were six ads each from two pro-Bush groups (Swift Boat Veterans for Truth and Progress for America), and 11 ads each from two pro-Kerry groups (The Media Fund and Move-On). As mentioned previously, the pro-Kerry 527 groups spent much more money and produced many more ads than did the pro-Bush 527 groups. This disparity is evidenced in the number of ads analyzed here: twelve ads supported Bush and twenty-two ads supported Kerry.

### Method

There were a number of different coding categories used in the analysis of these ads. Many of the categories were adapted from the widely used videostyle coding scheme developed by Kaid and her colleagues.[18] Included in the categories for analysis were: production attributes of the ads, ad focus (opponent or supported candidate), ad emphasis (issue or image), issues addressed, attacks made, appeals made, and strategies used.

The coding was performed by two coders using a common codebook and codesheet adapted and developed for this analysis. The average inter-coder reliability using Holsti's formula[19] was .878.

## RESULTS

### Production Attributes

The vast majority of the ads were thirty-seconds long. In fact, 28 (82.4 percent) of the ads were thirty seconds long or less. (This figure includes one 15-second ad.) The remaining six ads (17.6 percent) were sixty seconds long.

About two-thirds of the ads used two or more special effects, with twenty-nine using character generated text and fifteen making use of computer graphics. forty-seven percent of the ads analyzed used three or more special effects.

### Ad Focus

Each of the ads was coded as to whether it focused on presenting the supported candidate in a positive light or on presenting the opposed candidate in a negative light. Perhaps not surprisingly, the ads overall were predominantly negative, opponent-focused (N=29, 85.3 percent). Probably the most widely recognized ads from this campaign cycle were the Swift Boat Veterans for Truth ads that strongly attacked the character of Kerry. In fact, all six of the analyzed ads produced by this group were negative. The analyzed ads from the pro-Bush Progress for America, however, were evenly split with three negative and three positive ads. Among the positive ads was the ad often referred to as "Ashley" that centered around Bush's caring response to a girl whose mother had been killed on September 11.

The pro-Kerry groups also produced predominantly negative ads, with twenty of the twenty-two ads negatively focused. Sampled ads from The Media Fund and Move-On included ten negative ads each. One ad produced by The Media Fund was not candidate-focused at all, but rather it was an encouragement to vote (targeted at African-Americans). One ad produced by Move-On was positively focused in its support of Kerry.

These numbers present a stark contrast to the candidates' own ads, which previous analyses revealed to be split evenly between positive- and negative-focused ads.[20]

### Ad Emphasis

Although the image-oriented ads produced by the Swift Boat Vets garnered the most attention (and free airplay), the majority of the analyzed ads emphasized issues (N=21, 61.8 percent) rather than image (N=11, 32.4 percent). Perhaps as expected, the pro-Kerry ads were more likely to emphasize issues (18 of 22, or 81.8 percent), but the pro-Bush ads were more likely to emphasize image (8 of 12, or 66.7 percent). Because Bush was the sitting president, he had a track record on issues that he had dealt with as president. Critiques of his handling of these issues could serve as powerful critiques of his job performance. Kerry, on the other hand, played the role of challenger for the presidency. Negative portrayals of Kerry's image could serve to delegitimize him as a potential successor to the presidency.

### Issues Addressed

Twenty-four individual issues were coded for during this analysis. Most of the categorized issues did not turn up a single time in any of the ads in the sample. Issues that received zero mentions in the ads included: crime (not terrorism), drugs, children's issues, social policies, abortion, environmental issues, immigration, tobacco-related issues, taxes, welfare reform, education issues, civil rights, gun control, gay marriage or unions, federalism issues, and judicial activism. Many of these are normally considered "hot-button" issues that matter to the ideological bases of both parties. However, as expected, the Iraq war, terrorism, and the economy were the most commonly mentioned issues for the 527 groups in this campaign.

Almost one-quarter (N=8, 23.5 percent) of the analyzed ads mentioned the Iraq war. Most (75 percent) of these were ads from the pro-Kerry groups. The related issues of foreign affairs and defense spending were also mentioned in five (14.7 percent) of the ads.

The economy was mentioned in six (17.6 percent) of the analyzed ads. All of these were pro-Kerry ads. The related issue of budget deficits also received a mention in one ad (produced by Move-On).

Terrorism was mentioned in four (11.8 percent) of the ads. Three of these ads were produced by Progress for America, and one was produced by MoveOn. Receiving an equal number of mentions were health care issues. All four mentions were by pro-Kerry groups.

### Attacks

As indicated above, twenty-nine of the thirty-four ads analyzed were negative and focused on the opponent. Additionally, two more ads contained at least one or more negative attacks, even though the ads were primarily positive in focus. That represents a staggering 91.2 percent of the analyzed ads. These attacks were further categorized by type. Different types of attacks included attacks based on: personal characteristics, issue stances, affiliation/association, background/qualifications, performance in office, and political party.

The attacks in these ads were usually not based on personal characteristics. Except for the ads from the Swift Boat Vets, which all centered around attacks on Kerry's character, the rest of the analyzed ads with attacks tended to focus these attacks elsewhere. Overall, twelve ads (35.3 percent) of the sample featured an attack on personal characteristics. Half of these were the Swift Boat Vets ads. Only six of the other twenty-eight ads (21.4 percent) featured such an attack.

Also relatively uncommon were ads featuring attacks based on affiliation (N=6, 17.6 percent), background (N=2, 5.9 percent), or political party (N=0).

Most of the attacking ads contained attacks on a candidate's issue stances (N=18, 52.9 percent) or performance in office (N=26, 76.5 percent). MoveOn, in particular, featured an attack on Bush's performance in ten of the eleven ads analyzed from the group.

In all but one of the attacking ads analyzed, the attack was made directly on the opposed candidate. The one exception was the MoveOn ad "Swift Response," which directed its attack at the Swift Boat Vets in an effort to counteract their attack on Kerry.

## Appeals Made

Political ads can be designed to use at least three types of appeals: logical, emotional, and ethos (or credibility). The most frequently used type of political ad is a combination of logical and emotional, which is often referred to as a "dovetail" ad. This type provides a bit of factual information (or purported factual information) along with an emotional appeal. The combination can prove effective, and the ad does not run as much risk of being either too emotional (and therefore open to being labeled as manipulative) or too logical (and therefore being a bit dry or dull).

Of the ads analyzed, sixteen of them employed appeals to logic (47.1 percent). There were thirty-three with appeals to emotion (97.1 percent), and only five that employed appeals to credibility (14.7 percent). Several of the ads employed both logical and emotional appeals, with pro-Kerry groups making great use of that combination. The Media Fund produced eleven of the analyzed ads, and nine of them employed both logic and emotional appeals. All eleven of the MoveOn ads used emotional appeals, while four of them also used logical appeals. All of the Swift Boat Vets ads used emotional appeals, but not a single one used an appeal to logic. Two of the Swift Boat ads also contained an appeal to credibility, as the group sought to attack John Kerry's character.

## Strategies

Political campaigns can employ a variety of strategies, from those based on looking as if you are presidential material (such as being shown surrounded by the symbolic trappings of office) to painting an opponent as inexperienced and unqualified for the office. Finding the right strategy for a candidate can be hard, and campaign managers and consultants argue that it should be consistently employed.[21] Independent groups also often struggle when looking for the right strategy for their messages, as those strategies can have a direct bearing on the effectiveness of the ads themselves.

Of the ads analyzed, the two most frequently noted strategies were attacking the opponent's record and leadership. Both pro-Bush and pro-Kerry groups employed these strategies, which most often painted the opposing candidate in a negative light regarding past political decisions or leadership actions. Another common strategy, using surrogates to speak on behalf of a candidate, was found in only four of the ads analyzed. Of those, probably the best known example was the pro-Bush ad "Ashley," which featured a young girl whose mother died in the 9/11 attacks in New York. There were nine ads that used a strategy of questioning the opponent's competency, and seven ads featured a strategy of making a call for change. While most political ads are making some sort of appeal for change, these were ads with overt calls for change. Only two ads featured the strategy of using the symbolic trappings of office to promote a particular candidate. While this can be a common strategy for elected officials, it is less common for independent groups to pursue this strategy, as they are generally interested in promoting or opposing a particular issue or policy.

Very absent in the ads were appeals to traditional values, incumbency, or appealing to the political center. In fact, not a single ad contained any of these types of appeals. This could be attributed in part to the ads being produced by independent groups, rather than the candidate's organizations. While the goal of a candidate is to win office, the goals of independent organizations are somewhat different. Although they are oftentimes campaigning against a particular candidate, these groups usually have a particular issue that is of greatest interest to them, leaving them less likely to focus on appeals such as incumbency or the political center.

Overall, the strategies found in the ads reflect the already-noted tendency toward negative ads questioning the leadership and record of the opponent.

## CONCLUSION

The ads produced by the 527 groups for the 2004 presidential election differed from the ads produced by the campaigns. The 527-produced ads were much more likely to be negative than the campaign-produced ads. Thus, the ads were less supportive of a preferred candidate than they were hostile to an opposed candidate. This means that, even though the 527 ads were often issue-focused, they did very little to support the issues and platform of the preferred candidate. As mentioned above, this may have contributed to a general lack of message cohesiveness that cost Kerry's campaign more than it did Bush's.

The Nielsen Monitor-Plus and the Wisconsin Advertising Project, a political research group run by the University of Wisconsin's political science department, analyzed the campaigns and advertisements from both campaign committees and independent organizations and found that ads produced by 527 groups were predominately negative. In fact, the group found that independent groups aired "no purely positive spots" between September 24 and October 7, 2004.[22] Project researchers also found that candidate ads tended to be more positive than messages produced by political parties and independent groups (Wisconsin Advertising Project, 2009). This finding was echoed by a content analysis of television ads from the campaign which found that 81 percent of the independent group ads analyzed were negative, compared to only 50 percent of the candidate-sponsored ads.[23]

Several analysts note that candidates allowed the 527 groups to broadcast the most negative messages, which can be a big benefit for candidates because it helps them avoid the possible boomerang effect that negative advertising can sometimes cause.[24] The lax regulation of 527 groups, especially in the 2004 campaign, probably worked to each candidate's advantage, as the independent organizations—some of which had strong ties to individuals involved in presidential campaigns—produced hard-hitting ads which were aimed at undercutting the opponent's credibility.

The atmosphere in which these 527 groups grew and prospered was the direct result of campaign finance reform. Under this legislation, money that flowed into the political process was directed away from traditional organizations that are both beholden and accountable to the candidates' campaigns. The imposed distance between the 527 groups and the campaigns produced both independence for the groups and a firewall for the campaigns. Because the 527s were independent of the campaigns, the campaigns could not be held responsible for the actions of the 527s. Even though President Bush was challenged to repudiate the Swift Boat Veterans for Truth, his campaign suffered very little for their ads.

## NOTES

1. Pew Research Center, "Why Local TV Loves the Presidential Campaign," *Project for Excellence in Journalism,* 2 Jan. 2008, http://www.journalism.org/node/9164 (22 Dec. 2009).

2. Steve Rabinowitz. "Presidential TV Advertising Continues to Grow," Wisconsin Advertising Project, 8 Oct. 2008, wiscadproject.wisc.edu/wiscads_release_100808.pdf. (28 Dec. 2009).

3. Lynda Lee Kaid and Daniela V. Dimatrova, "The Television Advertising Battleground in the 2004 Presidential Election," *Journalism Studies* 6, no. 2 (2005): 165.

4. Center for Public Integrity, "State Secrets: Study to Examine 'Soft Money' in State Politics," 26 July 2001, www.publicintegrity.org/articles/entry/582/ (22 Dec. 2009).

5. L. Patrick Devlin, "Contrasts in Presidential Campaign Commercials of 2004," *American Behavioral Scientist* 49, no. 2 (October 2005): 279–313.

6. Center for Public Integrity, "Presidential Campaign Finance," 2005, www.gwu.edu/~action/2004/presfin04.html (21 Dec. 2009).

7. Committee on House Administration, Hearing on the Regulation of 527 Organizations, 20 April 2005, http://ftp.resource.org/gpo.gov/hearings/109h/21160.pdf (21 Dec. 2009).

8. Center for Public Integrity, "Presidential Campaign Finance."

9. Center for Public Integrity, "Presidential Campaign Finance."

10. Kaid and Dimatrova, "Television Advertising Battleground," 165–75.

11. Devlin, "Contrasts," 279–313.

12. Devlin, "Contrasts," 279–313.

13. Devlin, "Contrasts," 279–313.

14. Kaid and Dimatrova, "Television Advertising Battleground," 165–75.

15. Kaid and Dimatrova, "Television Advertising Battleground," 165–75.

16. Kaid and Dimatrova, "Television Advertising Battleground," 165–75.

17. Devlin, "Contrasts," 279–313.

18. Lynda Lee Kaid and Anne Johnston, *Videostyle in Presidential Campaigns.* (Westport, CT: Praeger/Greenwood, 2001).

19. Ole R. Holsti, *Content Analysis for the Social Sciences and Humanities* (Reading, MA: Addison-Wesley, 1969).

20. Kaid and Dimatrova, "Television Advertising Battleground," 165–75.

21. James Carville and Paul Begala. *Buck Up, Suck Up . . . and Come Back When You Foul Up* (New York: Simon and Schuster, 2003).

22. Wisconsin Advertising Project, "Obama Dominated Television Advertising in Ohio," 12 March 2008, wiscadproject.wisco.edu/wiscads_pressrelease_031208.pdf (24 June 2009).

23. Kaid and Dimitrova, "The Television Advertising Battleground," 165–75.

24. James King and Jason McConnell, "The Effect of Negative Campaign Advertising on Vote Choice: The Mediating Influence of Gender," *Social Science Quarterly*, 84, no. 4, (2003) 843–57.

## BIBLIOGRAPHY

Carville, James and Paul Begala. *Buck Up, Suck Up . . . and Come Back When You Foul Up* (New York: Simon and Schuster, 2003).

Center for Public Integrity. "State Secrets: Study to Examine 'Soft Money' in State Politics," 26 July 2001, www.publicintegrity.org/articles/entry/582/ (22 Dec. 2009).

Committee on House Administration, Hearing on the Regulation of 527 Organizations, 20 April 2005, http://ftp.resource.org/gpo.gov/hearings/109h/21160.pdf (21 Dec. 2009).

Devlin, L. Patrick. "Contrasts in Presidential Campaign Commercials of 2004," *American Behavioral Scientist* 49, no. 2 (October 2005): 279–313.

Holsti, Ole R. *Content Analysis for the Social Sciences and Humanities* (Reading, MA: Addison-Wesley, 1969).

Jasperson, Amy E. & David P. Fan. "An Aggregate Examination of the Backlash Effect in Advertising: The Case of the 1996 Senate Race in Minnesota." *Journal of Advertising*, 31 no. 1 (2002): 1–12.

Johnson-Cartee, Karen & Gary Copeland. "Southern voters' Reaction to Negative Political Ads Iin 1986 Election," *Journalism Quarterly*, 66, no. 4 (1989): 888–986.

Kaid, Lynda Lee and Anne Johnston. *Videostyle in Presidential Campaigns* (Westport, CT: Praeger/Greenwood, 2001).

Kaid, Lynda Lee and Daniela V. Dimatrova. "The Television Advertising Battleground in the 2004 Presidential Election." *Journalism Studies* 6, no. 2 (2005): 165–75.

King, James and Jason McConnell. "The Effect of Negative Campaign Advertising on Vote Choice: The Mediating Influence of Gender." *Social Science Quarterly*, 84, no. 4 (2003): 843–57.

Pew Research Center. "Why Local TV Loves the Presidential Campaign." Project for Excellence in Journalism, 2 Jan. 2008. http://www.journalism.org/node/9164 (22 Dec. 2009).

Rabinowitz, Steve. "Presidential TV Advertising Continues to Grow." Wisconsin Advertising Project, 8 Oct. 2008, wiscadproject.wisc.edu/wiscads_release_100808.pdf. (28 Dec. 2009).

# 7

# Silence Is(n't) Golden: Responding to 527 Ads

*Lauren Reichart Smith and Gary A. Copeland*

In 1804, Alexander Hamilton made disparaging remarks (or so it was reported) about Vice President Aaron Burr at a dinner party. Rather than launch an attack campaign, Burr instead challenged Hamilton to a duel. On July 11, 1804, the two met in a field in New Jersey. Ten paces were measured, the men took their places, and the word was given. Shots were fired, resulting in Hamilton falling to the ground after receiving a fatal wound.

Disparaging remarks about a candidate either by the opposition or by independent groups no longer call for a duel of honor with pistols or swords. However, just as in Hamilton and Burr's day, such disparaging action calls for a response. These days the field of honor is made up by the various media and the duelists' seconds have been replaced for the campaigns by 527s with an affinity to a particular candidate.

Political advertising typically comes in the forms of image, issue, and negative advertisements. Image ads are mini-biographies of the candidates. Their purpose is to introduce you to the life and background of the candidate. These ads are designed to increase name recognition and provide a positive story for the candidate. Issue ads deal strictly with political issues—usually the issues that are salient to the current political campaign and from the sponsoring candidate's perspective.

Negative ads are designed either to win favor with voters for the sponsoring candidate or to "drive up negatives" among the voters by pointing out the negative attributes of the opposing candidate. Negative ads (also referred to as attack ads or "mudslinging") point out weaknesses in the other candidate, both personally and professionally. Typically, attack ads are directed to policy issues and votes while mudslinging attacks the character of the opposition or of the opposition's family. Either form of negative ad may be run by a candidate or by a special interest group—and more recently, by 527 groups. The most famous negative political ad may be the "Daisy Girl" ad created by Tony Schwartz for Lyndon B. Johnson's 1964 presidential campaign. The spot depicts a little girl peeling petals off a daisy as she counts them. Her voice is replaced by a male voice counting down, and then a mock nuclear explosion. Over the visual of the explosion the voice of Lyndon Johnson is heard to say, "These are the stakes. To make a world in which all of God's children can live, or to go into the dark. We must either love each other, or we must die." The ad only aired one time, but that single airing made it one of the most controversial negative ads ever aired—despite the fact that President Johnson's opponent, Sen. Barry Goldwater, was never mentioned in the spot.

Prior to the 1980s, the typical ad campaign formula was issue and image ads first, then negative ads, and then image spots in the last few days before the election. This practice was abandoned after the 1980s with the norm shifting for many campaigns to increase negative ads and run them from the beginning of the campaign.[1] The increase in negative ads may have resulted from two factors: the increase in political advertising on television and the growth of independent action committees.[2] Sabato examined more than 1,100 political advertisements and concluded, "If there is a single trend obvious to most American consultants, it is the increasing proportion of negative political advertising. . . . At least a third of all spot commercials in recent campaigns have been negative, and in a minority of campaigns half or more of the spots are negative in tone or substance."[3] Although academic research has tried to determine the effectiveness of negative political advertising,[4] the conclusions have been mixed. Some research supports the use of negative advertising[5] while other research condemns its use.[6]

This ambiguity about effectiveness is not shared by political consultants. Many will admit that a negative ad may have some boomerang effect on the sponsoring candidate, but they maintain that the boomerang is significantly less than the hit taken by the target of the ad. In addition, the reduction in the sponsor's polling numbers usually rebounds within a few days while effective negative ads will affect the target's numbers for a longer period of time. Messages from negative ads are more pernicious than those from positive ads. With the right circumstances a negative political ad may be more influential, remembered longer, more easily recalled, and more persuasive than the information in a positive ad.[7]

Political ads that target an opponent's character are usually effective early in the campaign cycle. It is early that potential voters are attempting to know who a candidate is and what she or he stands for. Once the electorate has made a judgment about a candidate's persona, it is wise to move to issue attack ads. This strategy has been generally proven effective. The power of the negative ad comes from what Johnson-Cartee and Copeland refer to as the negativity effect.[8] They cite a large body of research that indicates that negative information is more powerful in the formation of judgments about a person than positive information. Negative information usually stands out in the minds of audiences. There is a body of evidence which suggests that negative information may be retrieved with greater ease than positive information.

The other advantage of negative ads is that they are often more cost efficient than positive spots. One of the reasons that challengers often adopt a negative approach in their advertising is because they do not have the finances to field a complete media campaign. The greater above-cited advantages of negative ads may make them the only practical approach for a relatively poorly funded campaign.

Ads from 527 groups differ in that they are sponsored by independent groups—not by opposing candidates. However, they may serve some of the same purposes of candidate-sponsored political ads in allowing voters to distinguish candidate qualities, positions, and performance.[9] A negative political ad may help voters differentiate candidate "qualities, positions, and performance more readily than would other types of political information that provide less explicit information. Also, the greater perceived differences between candidates may lead voters to greater attitude polarization regarding the candidates. That is, by discerning clear differences between candidates, voters may be more likely to strongly like one candidate while strongly disliking the other."[10]

There are various options that a candidate may employ in response to negative political ads from an opponent. The candidate may choose not to respond to the negative ad—adopting a position of silence. The candidate may decide to respond to the information in the ad directed against her/him. A response from the candidate's campaign may be an announcer-based message with the response being delivered by an unseen voice. The candidate may decide to come out and personally respond to the ad. Finally, it is possible for the candidate to have a surrogate—a spouse, child, or other trusted person—respond to the ad on the candidate's behalf.

## JOHN KERRY AND THE SWIFT BOAT VETERANS FOR TRUTH ADS: HOW NOT TO RESPOND

Sad, haunting music begins to play as a black and white picture of a young John Kerry fades up. A quote from his testimony on April 22, 1971, before the U.S. Senate Committee on Foreign Relations comes up, as the audio recording of the testimony plays at the same time. This particular advertisement is called "Sellout," and it was created by the Swift Boat Veterans for Truth.

| *Video* | *Audio* |
|---|---|
| Black and white photo of a young John Kerry, a quote in white font over the picture | John Kerry [VO]: They had personally raped, cut off ears, cut off heads . . . |
| Black and white photo of a young John Kerry, older gentleman in front of the picture—gfx identifies him as Joe Ponder, wounded in 1968 | Ponder [SOT]: The accusations that John Kerry made against the veterans who served in Vietnam was just devastating. |
| Black and white photo of a young John Kerry, a quote in white font over the picture | John Kerry [VO]: Randomly shot at civilians . . . |
| Black and white photo of a young John Kerry, older gentleman in front of the picture—gfx identifies him as Joe Ponder, wounded in 1968 | Ponder [SOT]: And it hurt even more than the physical wounds I had. |
| Black and white photo of a young John Kerry, a quote in white font over the picture | John Kerry [VO]: Cut off limbs, blown up bodies . . . |
| Black and white photo of a young John Kerry, older gentleman in front of the picture—gfx identifies him as Ken Cordier, P.O.W. | Cordier [SOT]: That was part of the torture to sign a statement that you committed war crimes. |
| Black and white photo of a young John Kerry, a quote in white font over the picture | John Kerry [VO]: Razed villages in a fashion reminiscent of Ghengis Kahn . . . |
| Black and white photo of a young John Kerry, older gentleman in front of the picture—gfx identifies him as Paul Galanti, P.O.W. | Galanti [SOT]: John Kerry gave the enemy, for free what I, and many of my comrades in North Vietnam in the prison camps, took torture to avoid saying. It demoralized us. |
| Black and white photo of a young John Kerry, a quote in white font over the picture | John Kerry [VO]: Crimes committed on a day to day basis. |

| | |
|---|---|
| Black and white photo of a young John Kerry, older gentleman in front of the picture—gfx identifies him as Ken Cordier, P.O.W. | Cordier [SOT]: He betrayed us in the past, how could we be loyal to him now? |
| Black and white photo of a young John Kerry, a quote in white font over the picture | John Kerry [VO]: Ravaged the countryside of South Vietnam . . . |
| Black and white photo of a young John Kerry, older gentleman in front of the picture—gfx identifies him as Paul Galanti, P.O.W. | Galanti [SOT]: He dishonored his country, and more importantly, the people he served with. |
| Fade to black and white picture of Kerry | Galanti [VO]: He sold them out, |
| Graphic of the Swift Boat slate | Narrator [VO]: The Swift Boat Veterans for Truth is responsible for this advertisement. |

This ad, along with several others, made up the Swift Boat Veterans for Truth ad campaign that repeatedly attacked Sen. John Kerry in the 2004 presidential election. Later rebranded as Swift Vets and POW's for Truth, this advocacy organization was formed in 2004 for the purpose of opposing Kerry's candidacy for the presidency. They began their ads on the premise that Kerry's conduct during the Vietnam war (which they alleged included withholding and distorting facts) made him unfit to serve as president.[11] The project was financed with a donation from Republican activist Sam Fox, and all public relations for the campaign were conducted by Arthur J. Finkelstein of Arthur J. Finkelstein and Associates, who has been noted for black-propaganda campaigns that are primarily character assassinations or smearing of a candidate.[12]

## TIMELINE

Swift Boat Veterans for Truth registered their Web site on April 14, 2004; went public at a news conference at the National Press Club on May 4, 2004; and then remained dormant until the debut of their first television ad in select markets in Ohio, West Virginia, and Wisconsin on August 5, 2004.[13] Three more ads from the group ran between August 20 and August 31. Prior to the television ad, the Swift Boat Vets issued a statement explaining their version of John Kerry's military history, including a picture that featured a group of soldiers, with most of the men shadowed, but John Kerry and three other men standing boldly out with the caption "John Kerry's Band of Brothers?"[14] The book *Unfit for Command: Swift Boat Veterans Speak Out Against John Kerry* (released in August, 2004) was written by Swift Boat Vets founder and spokesman Jerome R. Corsi. The book criticized Kerry's judgment in battle, his truthfulness, his entitlement to certain medals, and his later anti-war activities.

The first response came from the Kerry camp August 5th, the same day as the airing of the first television ad. However, the response was not to the potential voters, but to television station managers. John Kerry's general counsel faxed a letter to the station managers at the relevant stations stating that the ad was "an inflammatory, outrageous lie" and requesting that they "act immediately to prevent broadcast of this advertisement and deny any future sale of time."[15]

Since the ad was not run by a federal candidate, and instead run by an independent group, television stations were not required to broadcast it. According to Section 312 of the Federal Communications Act, "The [Federal Communications] Commission may revoke any station license . . . for willful or repeated failure to allow reasonable access to or to permit purchase of reasonable amounts of time for the use of a broadcasting station, other than a non-commercial educational broadcast station, by a legally qualified candidate for Federal elective office on behalf of his candidacy." Section 312 effectively requires broadcasters to sell time to federal candidates. The section does not make the same requirement for state and local candidates. A broadcast station could decide not to sell advertising time for a gubernatorial contest but would be required to do so for a person running for the House of Representatives. Also, non-candidate organizations such as 527s are not covered by the requirements of Section 312.[16]

Additionally, Section 315 states, "If any licensee shall permit any person who is a legally qualified candidate for any public office to use a broadcasting station, he shall afford equal opportunities to all other such candidates for that office in the use of such broadcasting station: *Provided*, That such licensee shall have no power of censorship over the material broadcast under the provision of this section. No obligation is hereby imposed under this subsection upon any licensee to allow the use of its station by any such candidate."[17] This rule applies only to ads run by qualified candidates—for example, if President Bush had run an ad on an ABC-affiliated station, that same station would have to make the same air time in a comparable time slot available to John Kerry for purchase. Although the ads from anyone who is not a candidate or a candidate's official campaign committee are subject to the same rules as any other commercial advertising, the case law for libel as applied to candidates in campaigns grants near immunity to the sponsor and the station. Given the relative dearth of libel cases involving broadcasters and 527-produced ads specifically, though, it is unclear whether the Kerry campaign could have prevailed in a libel suit by arguing that Section 315 does not apply to 527 groups.

Harsh criticism was later given to Kerry for how he chose to respond. With that first advertisement, Kerry threatened legal action, but never addressed the allegations made by the Swift Boat Vets. As stated above, the letter sent by his counsel was probably baseless and served only as an attempt at intimidation to the television stations—not even successful intimidation at that. During the days following this first ad, Kerry focused on criticizing President Bush for his reaction on the morning of 9/11. On August 10, a complaint was filed with the Federal Election Commission (FEC) by Democracy 21, The Campaign Legal Center, and The Center for Responsive Politics, which accused the Swift Boat Vets of illegally raising and spending soft money on ads to influence the 2004 presidential election.[18]

The Kerry campaign effectively responded with silence. While they maneuvered behind the scenes, the message to the voters was quiet. Although those people who liked the inside-baseball of campaigns knew of the legal machinations, the majority of voters knew only that people were essentially calling Kerry a liar and that he was not reacting. While all was quiet to the electorate, an argument was being held within the campaign itself. Some advisers counseled to keep quiet. The ad buy was relatively small. People would not believe the charges. To address the accusations in the ad would only provide them with credibility. Discussing the ad could turn the spot from being a 24- or 48-hour story in the news cycle to something that lasted longer. The other faction believed that a response was needed immediately. Ignoring the charges made people wonder if, in fact, the charges were true or at least partially true. The lack of response could also be interpreted as a lack of leadership or of resolve—an issue that the campaign was already dealing with.

Still not formally addressing the ad or the accusations contained within, the Kerry campaign announced on August 19, 2004, its own ad, titled "Rassmann." This ad featured Vietnam vet Jim Rassmann speaking about how Kerry "risked his life to save mine" by pulling him out of a river. It goes on to note how the Navy awarded Sen. Kerry the Bronze Star.

| *Video* | *Audio* |
|---|---|
| John Kerry talking to a group | John Kerry [VO]: I'm John Kerry and I approve this message. |
| Black and white video (blurred) of the Swift Boat Vets ad, graphic of text | Narrator [VO]: The people attacking John Kerry's war record are |

| | |
|---|---|
| that reads "The Attacks are Funded by Bush Supporters" | funded by Bush's big money supporters. |
| Footage from Vietnam—boats moving through water. | Narrator [VO]: Listen to someone who was there—the man whose life John Kerry saved. |
| Close up shot of Jim Rassmann, graphic with his name and "U.S. Army Special Forces, Vietnam" | Rassmann [SOT]: It blew me off the boat. |
| Footage from Vietnam—boats moving through water | All these Viet Kong were shooting at me. I expected I'd be shot when he pulled me out of the river. |
| Close up shot of Jim Rassmann | He risked his life to save mine. |
| Blurred shot of a document with the header "Department of the Navy" | Narrator [VO]: The Navy documented John Kerry's heroicism and awarded him the bronze star. |
| Black and white photo of John Kerry in his Naval uniform, with text that says "Read the Official Documents at JohnKerry.com" | |
| John Kerry, wearing a helmet, carrying a rifle, presumably in Vietnam, with text that says "Read the Official Documents at JohnKerry.com" | Today he still has shrapnel in his leg from Vietnam. |

Also on August 19, Kerry responded directly to the ad in a speech to the International Association of Firefighters' Convention in Boston. "Here's what you really need to know about them," Kerry said of the Swift Boat Vets. "They're funded by hundreds of thousands of dollars from a Republican contributor out of Texas. They're a front for the Bush campaign. And the fact that the president won't denounce what they're up to tells you everything you need to know—he wants them to do his dirty work . . . Of course, the president keeps telling people he would never question my service to the country. Instead, he watches as a Republican-funded attack group does just that. Well, if he wants to have a debate about our service in Vietnam, here is my answer: Bring it on."[19]

The following day, a second television ad from Swift Boat Vets began airing. Two days later, the Kerry campaign announced their second ad,

"Issues," which addressed the Swift Boat Vets' attack. Two more ads from the Swift Boat Vets ran before August ended, and only one more response came forth in this time period from John Kerry's campaign—a letter delivered to President Bush's ranch in Texas by former Senator Max Cleland and Jim Rassmann, asking the president to recognize the attempt at character assassination and condemn it publicly.[20] He did not condemn that specific ad; rather, he spoke out against 527 ads in general.

The campaign staff and John Kerry have been harshly criticized for their response to the Swift Boat Vets' charges. These charges dominated much of the political discussion in August 2004. The Kerry campaign was seen as too slow in their response. Their first response was to treat the book and the ads as an irritation—something that would go away if ignored. As talk continued and grew, the next step of the Kerry campaign was an attempt to discredit the Swift Boat Vets through threats of lawsuits against television stations that ran the ads, accusations of being funded by the Republican Party, and attacks on the character of one of the authors of the book, including the accusation that the other coauthor had a personal vendetta. They demanded the book be pulled from the shelves by the publisher.[21] Two steps in to their refutation, and the Kerry camp had yet to specifically address the charges—rather than face the accusation head on, they spent precious time and energy trying to discredit everyone involved with the attack campaign.

The Kerry campaign's final response came in an effort to brand the Swift Boat Vets as liars, hoping that if they repeated that mantra enough, the American people would come to accept it. This strategy failed to work for the Kerry campaign.[22] Most of the response to the Swift Boat charges came from the Democratic Party, rather than the Kerry campaign. The Democrats were the ones to call on President Bush to denounce the specific smear ad from the Swift Boat Vets, but the President would not, only rejecting 527 ads in general. It was also the Democratic Party, not the Kerry campaign that worked to find the connections between the Swift Boat group and the Bush campaign staff and associates.[23]

The response by the Kerry campaign was one of hesitation followed by an appearance of avoiding having to face the charges directly. The actions by the DNC on Kerry's behalf along with appealing to the opponent made the Kerry campaign appear weak and powerless. This appearance would play into the meme that the Republicans were attempting to create about Kerry thus providing even greater power to their attacks.

Sen. Kerry has also been criticized for bringing the attack upon himself by bringing up his service in Vietnam. During the 2004 campaign, one of the hot button issues was the highly contested war in Iraq. When considering how unpopular the war was at that time, the war in Vietnam and Kerry's service in the war could be considered to be highly relevant when spun in a certain light. The strategy behind Kerry's message about his service in

Vietnam was to prove that he would be better suited to be commander-in-chief; some took the message to be nothing but bragging that he was more manly than President Bush.[24] When sending out the message that his service proves him to be more of a man, one wonders how the opposition could not attack him on this point.

The failure of John Kerry to immediately denounce the ads as false ultimately resulted in a questioning of his character, the factor that ended up turning the tide against him, with the thought being that the way he handled his response to the Swift Boat ads only served to show him as unable to be truthful about the real relevance of his Vietnam experience in relation to the Iraq war.[25]

An interesting comparison is found in the responses by Sen. Kerry and then Sen. Obama to the respective books written by Jerome R. Corsi. As noted prior, Corsi's book *Unfit for Command* served as one of the starting points for the Swift Boat Vets ads, and the Kerry campaign never directly addressed the book, the accusations in the book, or the accusations made by the Swift Boat Vets. In 2008, Corsi released a new book, *The Obama Nation,* intended to oppose the Obama presidency. The book attacked Obama's political ideologies, alleged inexperience, collaboration with terrorist groups, past drug use, and corruption.[26] In contrast to Kerry's response, the Obama response was swift and immediate. A 40-page response was issued on the campaign Web site devoted to fighting smear campaigns, and a press release was issued in the *New York Times* that stated the book was a series of lies, and that the response to the smears would be forceful. The difference in responses is obvious; what is interesting to point out is that after *The Obama Nation* was released, Sen. Kerry launched a Web site also devoted to discrediting the claims.

## RESPONDING TO NEGATIVE ADS

### The "Rovian Way"

The "Rovian Way" has become a common phrase in mainstream politics. Karl Rove served as the Deputy Chief of Staff for President George W. Bush until 2007. The majority of his career prior to the White House was spent as a political consultant. Rove worked almost exclusively with Republicans, including presidents George W. Bush, George H.W. Bush, and Ronald Reagan, as well as select senators and congressmen. Rove was described by *Time* magazine's White House correspondent as the most influential and important political consultant to a president anyone has ever seen.[27] Although Rove may be best known for his contribution to the close presidential victory in 2000, the closest race he ever ran was the 1994 Alabama

Supreme Court race. At that time, the state of Alabama was a resolutely Democratic state. A group called the Business Council of Alabama, after observing that Rove had been able to achieve success with the same scenario in Texas several years prior, asked Rove to help Republican candidates get elected to the Supreme Court of Alabama. Because of the strong Democratic leanings of the state, judicial races prior to that time were done with little campaigning.

When Rove was hired, the nature of judicial campaigns in Alabama changed. Rove employed tactics that "demoniz(ed) Democrats as pawns of the plaintiffs' bar and stok(ed) populist resentment with tales of outrageous verdicts."[28] Rove used cases presided over and verdicts handed down by incumbent Democratic justices that he could spin as outrageous verdict cases. The public took notice, and became enraged. One particular smear ad run by the Republican candidate garnered national attention. The final two weeks of the campaign featured a barrage of attack ads against the Democratic candidates. When the unofficial tally on voting day showed a Democrat victory, Rove demanded a recount. He sent staffers to observe the recount and hired investigators to find evidence of fraud. The campaign staff began telling tales of fraudulent activity, enabling Rove's Republican candidate to declare the election was being stolen. The recount lasted for a year—at the end, the United States Supreme Court was called in to make the final ruling, and Rove's Republican candidate was appointed to the Alabama Supreme Court.

Rove's style of politics was to run a highly organized yet ruthless campaign, and that style usually yielded him victory. His name is often associated with dirty tricks, investigations that just happen to happen at just the right time, and electoral legerdemain.[29] Diverting the focus from the issues that could be discussed in favor of assassinating the character of your opponent at every available opportunity has been dubbed the "Rovian" style of politics.[30] The personal attack and assault effectively becomes the issue at hand, and is strictly geared toward eliminating the substance of any political argument. Journalists then pick up on the personal attack, because mudslinging is easier to report on than issues of policy. Despite the fact that his style made him popular within the media, in the circles of Washington his style was not favored. Personal attacks and diversion from the issues earned him numerous enemies through insults he hurled at members of Congress and threats made to his own staff. Rove is connected to accusations of a fraudulent bugging incident in his own office in Texas in 1986, and his tactics have been condemned as corrupting the democratic process in the United States. Democrat Gary Mauro, who lost to George W. Bush in the 1998 Texas gubernatorial election, said of Rove, " . . . he's an evil man. When we [the Democrats] had the U.S. attorney's and the FBI, we didn't go sit down with the FBI and tell them to go get someone. Karl Rove thought that was always OK. And that's why I think he's evil. He corrupts the system in a basic way."[31]

## Inoculation

Inoculation theory derives from the idea that an early weak attack can make a prior held belief stronger. A campaign may have the ability to, in essence, warn a candidate's supporters of an upcoming attack in order for the supporters to withstand the attack and maintain a positive attitude toward the candidate.[32] The most common analogy associated with inoculation theory is that of giving a vaccination to help a person ward off a disease. McGuire explained, "the person is typically made resistant to some attacking virus by pre-exposure to a weakened dose of the virus. This mild dose stimulates his defenses so that he will be better able to overcome any massive viral attack to which he is later exposed, but it is not so strong that this pre-exposure itself will cause the disease."[33] For example the Republican Party could send out literature to potential Republican voters warning them that the Democrats are likely to attack the Republican candidate on various issues. The literature would provide a weak version of the attacks which would engage the voter in a process of thinking about the issue and mentally defending the held position. Then when the real Democrat attack comes, the potential Republican voter would fight it off. Previous research has shown that inoculation is a viable strategy for building resistance against the influence of political attack messages.[34]

Inoculation is not limited to campaign races. In looking back over President Clinton's terms one can see several clear examples of how the Clinton strategists utilized inoculation theory while Clinton served in office. Democrats were inoculated against charges that Clinton was soft on crime when Clinton declared support for the death penalty and three-strike laws, Clinton's stance on family values, school uniforms, and the V-chip served to inoculate Democrats when his images was deemed as "countercultural McGovernism," and his signing a 1996 Republican-backed welfare bill helped inoculate Democrats when Clinton was charged with being soft on welfare mothers.[35]

Inoculation theory proves most useful in the world of televised debates. A 2006 study by An and Pfau showed the effectiveness of using inoculation to resist the influence of attack messages utilized during debates. Their research found that supporters of one candidate that had been inoculated with the weaker version of a character attack were more resistant to the actual attacks launched by the opposing candidate.[36] Previous research indicated that inoculation worked best on a passive receiver, and thus television was an ideal ground for its use.[37] However, more recent literature suggests that an active participant may be more receptive to inoculation.[38] Pfau, Van Brockern, and Geenkang suggest that the point of inoculation is to get people to think for themselves. When people have to go through the active process of generating their own ideas and thoughts, they will develop stronger attitudes, beliefs, and behaviors than a person who is, in essence, spoon fed the information.

## Strategic Silence in Politics

In the days of elementary school, children tease each other on the playground. The children getting teased have a couple of options to defend themselves: fight back, ignore it, or get someone else to fight their battle for them. Washington, D.C. is essentially a grown-up playground, and attack ads are the politicians' versions of playground teasing. The options for fighting back remain the same.

Strategic silence in politics was effectively defined as "a refusal of a public figure to communicate verbally when that refusal (1) violates expectations, (2) draws public attribution of fairly predictable meanings, and (3) seems intentional and directed at an audience."[39] In Brummett's later conclusions, it was deemed that silence is not an effective political strategy for candidate-elects.[40] By refusing to speak out, the voter is left with the responsibility to interpret the actions of the political candidate, and people will then create their own explanations for the silence.[41] Americans admire a person who fights back and stands up for him or herself, thus, if the candidate does not fight back against the attack, then they are essentially saying that they are guilty of what they are being accused of. Some candidates may see themselves as taking the high road and not dignifying the attack with a response, however, voters can perceive this as the candidate being on the defensive.

There are several reasons a candidate or a campaign may opt for the strategy of silence. The first is that they do not want to give the attack ad any more attention than it may have already received. By responding, not only do they potentially prolong the exposure of the ad, but giving the attack ad attention may give the impression that the attack is one that is credible. Another reason they may choose to stay silent is because they may feel that dignifying the attack with a response is beneath them. Candidates may also choose to stay silent because they put faith in the assumption that people know the attack is a lie.

The 1990 race for governor of Alabama is a solid example of a candidate staying silent in the face of an attack ad. The 1990 gubernatorial race featured Republican Guy Hunt (the incumbent) and Democrat Paul Hubbard. The Republican Party sought to keep the power of the governor in Republican hands, while the Democrats positioned the need for a "New South" governor that would bring change to the state. The attack ad produced by Guy Hunt's campaign, accused Hubbard (who was also the current director of the state teachers association) of deliberately recruiting homosexual candidates for jobs within the schools. After the ad aired, Hubbard wanted to take immediate action and call Hunt a liar, but Hubbard's media consultant advised Hubbard to take no action. The ad was believed to be so heinous that it would backfire on Hunt and ensure victory for Hubbard. Hubbard stayed silent, and instead the campaign decided to create a "talking head" ad featuring Hubbard's minister responding on his behalf. The surrogate defense ad wasn't seen until four days after the initial broadcast of the Hunt commercial. The end result was a drastic drop in the polls for Hubbard, and a victory for Hunt.

There are definite problems that come with deciding to stay silent. The primary problem is that voters do not believe in the strategy of silence. As mentioned above, the American myth says that you stand up for yourself in the face of bullies. The (wo)manly thing to do in these attack situations is to fight back, not stay silent. Leaders are supposed to stand up for the truth. Presidents, especially, will have to deal with leaders, some dangerous, and our belief is that our President will fight for us, not remain silent. Although politicians may view an attack ad as a desperate measure on the part of the other candidate that no one believes, voters tend to think that if the ad wasn't true, the candidate would say so, because no one in their right mind would just ignore a wrongful attack.

Secondly, although the idea to not talk about the ad and draw further attention to it might be sound in theory, in reality, it can backfire very quickly on a candidate because if they decline to talk about it, there is a good chance that someone else will—especially if it looks like the attack is working. In this instance, rather than just dealing with the attack ad, the candidate may be forced to deal with additional backlash from news or media outlets talking about the ad.

John Kerry took the route of silence when dealing with the Swift boat attack ads. The biggest form of response from the Kerry campaign with regards to the ads was eliciting former crewmembers of Kerry to give interviews on his behalf—and there was a very small number of those. But once again, Kerry is seen turning to others to defend him against the charges. The ads first aired on August 4, 2004—after almost three weeks of silence, Kerry finally responded to the ads, and his response at this point was to chastise the use of a front group—not a response that would deem the group's claim's untrue. It could be said that Kerry's response at this point was still him remaining silent on the issues. By attacking the source of the ad, and not the claims of the ad, Kerry left the door open for voters to wonder if the issues were not true, why Kerry was not vigorously standing up for himself.

### Speaking Out

Speaking out is the antithesis of remaining silent, and can come in a variety of forms. The most common include confession/redemption, sanctimonious admission, denial/attack campaign, counterattacks, refutation, obfuscation, and counter-imaging.[42] Although each individual method has its own advantages and disadvantages, it is important to remember that there is no single correct way to refute a negative ad. Since negative ads can attack either character or policy (or both), sometimes the most effective speaking out strategy will employ more than one of the above listed tactics. However, choosing to engage in defense comes with its own set of liabilities, including devoting resources to issues that may be better suited to the opponent, and the fact that responding to the ad means having to acknowledge it, which may serve as a reminder to voters about the weakness the candidate is trying to defend themselves against.[43]

Confession and redemption brings to mind a church confessional draped in a heavy curtain with whispered voices declaring their sins and asking for forgiveness. Take away the church and the heavy curtain and replace it with televisions and the voting public, and you have confession and redemption as a response to an attack ad. In this tactic, a candidate essentially admits to the allegations of the attack and asks for forgiveness. Since religious teachings proclaim that confession is a route to redemption, the voting public is more tolerant of a candidate who can admit to their mistakes and apologize and are more apt to forgive that candidate.[44]

Sanctimonious admission brings confession up to a new level. Not only does the candidate admit to their mistakes in this tactic, but they do not apologize for what they are being accused of. Quite the opposite—they take the stance of saying if they had to go through the process all over again, they would not change their actions. According to Johnson-Cartee and Copeland, this strategy gives a candidate two advantages: a) it allows the voting public to see a candidate stand firm to their position and not cave to political pressure, and b) it places the heat back on the original attackers because the issue is now considered desirable by the voters.

A denial/attack campaign is a two-step measure that involves first denying the claims in the negative ad, then following up by attacking the opposing campaign for being involved in dirty campaign tactic.[45] The more common term of this strategy is "mudslinging," which came to its name by being described as "as American as Mississippi mud."[46] In other words, mudslinging in politics is quite common. The denial/attack tactic has the advantage of quickly refocusing the voters on a new attack against the opposition.

A counterattack was originally defined as a military tactic where a group being attacked could strike at the right moment, usually in a surprise move, and gain the upper hand of the battle. A political counterattack is an ad that responds to negative ads by attacking the sponsor of the originating ad.[47] Kern[48] attributes the strategy to a fighting fire with fire measure. Johnson-Cartee and Copeland[49] state that a counterattack usually serves to increase the negativity that already exists in the campaign, and in order to have an effect, the counterattack must be stronger than the original attack ad. Mutz, Sneiderman, and Brody found that voters generally find direct responses to negative or attack ads more persuasive than counterattack ads.[50]

Refutation has been found to be the optimal reactive response because voters are most likely to believe a refutation response.[51] Merriam-Webster defines refuting as "to prove wrong by argument or evidence; show to be false or erroneous."[52] In the refutation strategy, the politician bases their response on solid evidence that is irrefutable.[53] When evidence is irrefutable, it makes it impossible to argue against. Just as is the case with libel, truth is always the best defense.

Obfuscation can be used for a variety of purposes, but in the context of political campaigning, it deals with a politician essentially doing a card trick to divert attention. Since obfuscation does not contain any actual evidence, the politician cannot deny the charges. Instead, they launch a response that is filled with assertions and protestations that they pass off as evidence to in attempt to avoid denying the attack.[54] This approach may make use of the nondenial denial. Let's say a person is charged with falsifying her resume which claims she graduated Oxford. The candidate's response might be, "I'm startled that the opposition would make such a claim. We have sent to Oxford today to get an official copy of the transcript." Sounds like the charge is denied, but not really. There was no specific claim made that the person had a degree. She only said they sent for a transcript not that a transcript exists. Finally, counterimaging (also known as reframing) allows the attacked candidate to change the focus in some way. When reframing is referred to in film, it talks about changing the angle on a camera shot without making a cut in order to give a new perspective on the scene. Counterimaging does the same type of duty—it attempts to reframe the public persona of the candidate that was attacked by providing a new perspective on them.[55]

## Timing

Timing plays an important role in responding to an attack ad. The longer a politician sits silently on an attack of his character, the more guilty he begins to look. Responses to negative attack ads should be immediate.

The presence of YouTube has helped speed up the time between attack and response. The problem of distribution of political ads and the purchasing of time on television and radio stations that could cause an additional twenty-four to forty-eight hour delay can be relieved through putting up the ad on YouTube and alerting the news media. For major contests, people may be seeing a copy of the response ad on the news before it appears in a station break.

## 527 ADS RUNNING IN THE 2008 PRESIDENTIAL ELECTION

Despite the criticisms of 527 ads during the final months of the 2004 presidential election, their presence continued and was employed in the 2008 presidential election. As the 2008 election entered the final few weeks prior to the November election, 527 ads continued to run, though not without some controversy. In fact, the term "Swift boating" took its place as a part of the election discourse. A June 2008 article in the New York *Times* stated, "'Swift boat' has become the synonym for the nastiest of campaign smears, a shadow that hangs over the presidential race as pundits wait to proclaim that the Swiftboating has begun and candidates declare that they will not be Swiftboated."[56] Candidates in the 2008 election used the term "Swift boating" when discussing a harsh attack made by a political opponent. It doesn't seem to matter if the attack is personal in nature or deals with a candidate's policy issue. The term has become synonymous with the idea of smearing someone's name; in fact, the term has extended beyond the political arena in some cases, with "Swift boating" being linked to names like Cindy Sheehan and WalMart. There has been opposition to the use of this term to define a smear technique, both from media commentators and the Swift Boat Veterans.[57]

A 527 group gets its name from its tax-exempt status under the United States tax code. Organizations that fall under the 527 status do not spend money on ads that directly support a particular candidate, they avoid regulation by the Federal Election Commission. An important point to remember with regards to 527 ads is that their purpose is to focus on the issues, not to attack or defend a specific candidate. The Swift Boat Veterans for Truth group and the group MoveOn were both fined by the Federal Election Commission in 2004 for specifically attacking the candidates and failing to focus on the issues. Another point to consider within the 2008 election is that the candidates took to calling all independently funded groups "527's," but in the strictest sense, not all of the groups the candidates label as 527 groups fall legally under that tax-exempt status. The Federal Election Commission ruled in 2004 that 527 groups should not be regulated under the rules of campaign finance. However, following the 2004 election, the Federal Election Commission ruled that ads that attacked a candidate's character or qualifications for the office sought would be illegal for 527s to run.[58] Specific character assassinations would have to be left up to Political Action Committees, and those groups have been lumped in by the candidates to the 527 group.

The first major 527 ad of the 2008 campaign was produced by the group PoliticalHitman.com, attacked Senator Obama and Senator Clinton, and focused on the topic of religion. Groups such as the American Leadership Project, Freedom's Watch, the National Campaign Fund, the Alliance for a New America, Moveon.org, and VoteVets.org all produced ads that ran between March and September of 2008. Ads showcased issues such as the economy, the mortgage crisis, high gas prices, religion, and the war in Iraq. The early ads were primarily focused on Senators McCain, Clinton, and Obama, but Senator Edwards was the target of one.

As stated previously, the rules regarding what 527 ads can cover have changed since the 2004 election. The majority of the groups running independent ads do not classify themselves under the 527 status, and raise their money from various donations. By not classifying themselves as 527 groups, they avoid the ruling set forth by the Federal Election Commission, and can create and run ads that attack a candidate's character and qualifications. They also avoid having to disclose how much money they receive, or how they decide to spend it. Operating outside of the rules that govern 527 groups and political action committees, independent groups are free to conduct their own polling. They can also design their ads in a way that will complement what the party they support is doing; on the flip side, with no governing body to be accountable to, then can also engage in the typical dirty politics that candidates would not want to be associated with.

Both Senators McCain and Obama voiced their disproval over independent groups and the attack ads that they could potentially run. In August of 2007, Senator Obama advised his donors to "Get involved in the campaign that we've set up, that is aboveboard, that is transparent, that is legal, and I think if people channel their energies in that way, we'll all be better off."[59] Senator Obama was very explicit in his instructions to his donors that they not give money to the independent groups, and he even threatened to cut off contact with any donor that decided to support an independent group. Senator McCain actually condemned the Swift Boat Veteran ads in 2004, and asked that President Bush do the same. Though the president never condemned the ads, he did propose a plan to work with Senator McCain to take legal action against the independent groups. McCain was responsible for the writing of the law that required disclosure by 527 groups that went into effect after the 2004 election; in the 2008 campaign, he again condemned the independent groups, but followed that up by saying he couldn't be a referee for their ads and content.[60]

What independent groups had on their side in the 2008 election—besides the power of independent money—was the ability to spread their messages more quickly and to a much wider audience than they were able to in 2004. Viral marketing strategies allow for a video or ad to be spread rapidly and to a large audience for virtually no cost. There is no ad buy for "YouTube." A 2008 Washington Post article detailed how an anonymous chain email that contained a fake biographical sketch of Senator Obama quickly became one of the most effective Internet attacks of the 2008 presidential season.[61] Danielle Allen, the subject of the article and a political theorist at the Institute for Advanced Study, points out that refuting smear campaigns on the Internet are not as easy as refuting traditional smear campaigns; candidates now are faced with things like source anonymity and technical efficiency that allow a smear campaign—true or not—to be spread like wildfire.

## CONCLUSION

Negative political advertising has become a prominent factor in political campaigns. This chapter outlines both potential responses to negative political ads, as well as what a 527 ad is and how it differs from a campaign sponsored negative advertisement. The presidential campaign of Senator John Kerry could be used as a study in how not to respond to negative political advertisements. Though there is no clear-cut formula and specific model to follow when responding to negative ads, one thing is certain—silence is not the answer.

## NOTES

1. W.H. Chang, J.J. Park, and S.W. Shim, "Effectiveness of Negative Political Advertising," *Web Journal of Mass Communication Research*, 2, no. 1 (1998).
2. G.M. Garramone, C.K. Atkin, B.E. Pinkleton, and R.T. Cole, "Effects of Negative Political Advertising on the Political Process," *Journal of Broadcasting & Electronic Media* 34, no. 3 (1990): 299–311.
3. Larry Sabato, *The Rise of Political Consultants: New Way of Winning Elections* (New York: Basic Books, 1981), 165.
4. S.F. Tinkham and R.A. Weaver-Lariscy, "A Diagnostic Approach to Assessing the Impact of Negative Political Television Commercials." *Journal of Broadcasting & Electronic Media* 37 (1993): 377–99.
5. S. Ansolabehere, and S. Iyengar, *Going Negative: How Political Advertisements Shrink and Polarize the Electorate* (New York: Free Press, 1997).
6. M. Basil, C. Schooler, and B. Reeves, "Positive and Negative Political Advertising: Effectiveness of Ads and Perceptions of Candidates," in *Psychological Process*, edited by F. Biocca (Hillsdale, NJ: Lawrence Erlbaum, 1991).
7. Karen Johnson-Cartee and Gary Copeland, *Combating Negative Advertising: Proactive and Reactive Strategies* (Westport, CT: Praeger, 1997).
8. Johnson-Cartee and Copeland, *Combating Negative*.
9. Chang, Park and Shim, Effectiveness of Negative.
10. G.M. Garramone, C.K. Atkin, B.E. Pinkleton, and R.T. Cole, "Effects of Negative Political Advertising on the Political Process." *Journal of Broadcasting & Electronic Media* 34, no. 3 (1990): 299–311.
11. Multiple. "Swift Veterans Letter to John Kerry," (2004), horse.he.net/~swiftpow/article.php?story=20040629220813790 (21 May 2008).

12. J. Halper, "Dirty Politics." In *Flashpoint*: KPFA, 2006.

13. "Swift Liars: Kerry-Edwards Campaign Response," n.d., In www.democraticunderground.com/discuss/duboard.php?az=view_oet&address=358x25 (23 May 2008).

14. "Swift Boat Vets and POWS for Truth '527' Political Organization Filing Information" (n.d.).

15. M. Elias, and J. Sandler. "Re: Swift Boat Veterans for Truth," www.gwu.edu/%7Eaction/2004/ads04/dem080504ltrswift.html (26 May 2008).

16. Section 312 of the Federal Communications Act of 1934. www.fcc.gov/mb/policy/political/candrule.htm (22 Dec. 2009).

17. FCC.gov

18. G. Herbert, "Campaign Finance Groups File FEC Complaint Charging 'Swift Boat Veterans for Truth' Is Violating Federal Campaign Finance Laws," www.gwu.edu/%7Eaction/2004/ads04/sbvtcomplaint.html (27 May 2008).

19. Kerry-Edwards 2004 Campaign Ads. www.cbsnews.com/elements/2004/03/04/in_depth_politics/videoarchive603962_0_2_page.shtml (13 June 2008).

20. E.M. Appleton, "Some Responses to The "Swift Boat Veterans for Truth Ad," (2004), www.gwu.edu/%7Eaction/2004/ads04/swiftadresponse.html (22 May 2008).

21. J.E. O'Neill and J.L. Corsi. "Advantage Swift Vets," (2004), http://www.combatvetsagainstkerry.com/unfit_epilogue.pdf. (24 May 2008).

22. O'Neill and Corsi, "Advantage Swift."

23. Appleton, "Some Responses."

24. Frank Rich., "How Kerry Became a Girly-Man," *New York Times*, September 5, 2004.

25. R. Meister, "What Is to Be Done? Thinking Politically About the 2004 Election," *Theory & Event* 8, no. 2 (2005).

26. J.R. Corsi, *The Obama Nation: Leftist Politics and the Cult of Personality* (New York: Simon & Schuster, 2008).

27. J. Dymond, "Who Runs the Bush White House?" Review of Reviewed Item. BBC News, (2001), news.bbc.co.uk/1/hi/world/americas/1304014.stm.

28. J. Green, "Karl Rove in a Corner," *Atlantic Monthly*, 2004.

29. Green, "Karl Rove."

30. M. Bai, "Rove's Way," *New York Times*, 2002.

31. Mauro, 2002, as quoted in Green, 2004.

32. Karen Johnson-Cartee and Gary Copeland, *Negative Political Advertising: Coming of Age*, (Mahwah, NJ: Lawrence Erlbaum, 1991).

33. W.J. McGuire, "Inducing Resistance to Persuasion: Some Contemporary Approaches," in *Advances in Experimental Social Psychology*, edited by L. Berkowitz (New York: Academic, 1964), 200.

34. M. Pfau and M. Burgoon. "Inoculation in Political Campaign Communication." *Human Communication Research* 15 (1988): 91–111. M. Pfau, H.C. Kenski, M. Nitz, and J. Sorenson, "Efficacy of Inoculation Strategies in Promoting Resistance to Political Attack Messages: Application to Direct Mail," *Communication Monographs* 57 (1990): 1–12. M. Pfau, D. Park, R.L. Holbert, and J. Cho, "The Effects of Party- and Pac-Sponsored Issue Advertising and the Potential of Inoculation to Combat Its Impact on the Democratic Process," *American Behavioral Scientist* 44 (2001): 2379–97.

35. Barry Bluestone and Jonathan Chait "Conversation: Clinton's Bequest Reconsidered. American Prospect," 11, no. 4, (2000): 18–25.

36. C. An and M. Pfau, "The Efficacy of Inoculation in Televised Political Debates," *Journal of Communication* 54, no. 3 (2006): 421–36.

37. Johnson-Cartee and Copeland, *Negative Political Advertising*.

38. Pfau, Van Bockern, & Geenkang, in press.

39. B. Brummett, "Towards a Theory of Silence as a Political Strategy," *Quarterly Journal of Speech* 66 (1980): 289–303, 289.

40. Johnson-Cartee and Copeland, *Negative Political Advertising*.

41. Brummett, "Towards a Theory."

42. Johnson-Cartee and Copeland, *Combating Negative Advertising*.

43. W.L. Benoit, J.P. McHale, G.J. Hansen, P.M. Pier, and J.P. McGuire, *Campaign 2000: A Functional Analysis of Presidential Campaign Discourse* (Lanham, MD: Rowman & Littlefield, 2003).

44. Johnson-Cartee and Copeland, *Combating Negative Advertising*.

45. Johnson-Cartee and Copeland, *Combating Negative Advertising*.

46. W. Goodman, "The Airwaves: A Few Ideas for the Next Election," Review of Reviewed Item, *New York Times*, 1996, www.nyu.edu/gsas/dept/politics/seminars/russian5.pdf.

47. R. Baukus, J.G. Payne, and M. Reisler. "Negative Polispots: Mediated Argument in the Political Arena," in *Argument and Social Practice: Proceedings of the Fourth Sca/Afa Conference on Argumentation*, edited by J.R. Cox, M.O. Sillars and G.B. Walker (Annandale, VA: Speech Communication Association, 1985), 236–52.

48. M. Kern, *Thirty-Second Politics: Political Advertising in the Eighties* (New York: Praeger, 1989).

49. Johnson-Cartee and Copeland, *Negative Political Advertising*.

50. D.C. Mutz, P.M. Sniderman, and R.A. Brody. *Political Persuasion and Attitude Change* (Ann Arbor: University of Michigan Press, 1996).

51. Johnson-Cartee and Copeland, *Combating Negative Advertising*. G.M. Garramone, *Voter Responses*. Barbara G. Salmore and Stephen A. Salmore, Candidates, *Parties, and Campaigns: Electoral Politics in America*. (Washington, DC: CQ Press, 1985).

52. MerriamWebster.com.

53. M.J. McGuire, "Inducing Resistance to Persuasion: Some Contemporary Approaches," in *Advances in Experimental Social Psychology*, edited by L. Berkowitz (New York: Academic, 1964), 191–229. James McCroskey. "A summary of Experimental Research on the Effects of Evidence in Persuasive Communication." *Quarterly Journal of Speech*, 55, (1969): 169–76. James McCroskey. "The effects of Evidence as an Inhibitor of Counter-Persuasion," *Speech Monographs*, 37, no. 3 (1970): 188–93.

54. Johnson-Cartee and Copeland, *Combating Negative Advertising*.

55. Johnson-Cartee and Copeland, *Combating Negative Advertising*.

56. K. Zernike, "Veterans Long to Reclaim the Name 'Swift Boat'," Review of Reviewed Item. *New York Times*, no. (2008), www.nytimes.com/2008/06/30/us/politics/30swift.html?_r=1&oref=slogin.

57. M. Rosen,"Story Is None Too 'Swift'," Review of Reviewed Item. *Rocky Mountain News*, (2006), www.rockymountainnews.com/drmn/opinion_columnists/article/0,2777,DRMN_23972_5096616,00.html. Zernike, Veterans Long.

58. M. Luo, "Ready to Attack Obama, If Some Money Arrives," Review of Reviewed Item. *New York Times*, (2008), www.nytimes.com/2008/06/21/us/politics/21ads.html?hp=&pagewanted=all.

59. P. Overby, "Political Ads from '527' Groups Get Cold Shoulder," Review of Reviewed Item. *NPR*, (2008), www.npr.org/templates/story/story.php?storyId=90907225.

60. Overby, "Political Ads."

61. M. Mosk, "An Attack That Came out of the Ether: Scholar Looks for First Link in E-Mail Chain About Obama," Review of Reviewed Item. *Washington Post*, (2008), http://www.washingtonpost.com/wpdyn/content/article/2008/06/27/AR2008062703781.html?sid=ST2008062703939&pos=.

## BIBLIOGRAPHY

An, C., and M. Pfau. "The Efficacy of Inoculation in Televised Political Debates." *Journal of Communication* 54, no. 3 (2006): 421–36.

Ansolabehere, S., and S. Iyengar. *Going Negative: How Political Advertisements Shrink and Polarize the Electorate*. New York: Free Press, 1997.

Appleton, E.M. 2004. Some Responses to The "Swift Boat Veterans for Truth" Ad, gwu.edu/%7Eaction/2004/ads04/swiftadresponse.html (accessed May 22, 2008).

Bai, M. "Rove's Way." *New York Times*, 2002.

Basil, M., C. Schooler, and B. Reeves. "Positive and Negative Political Advertising: Effectiveness of Ads and Perceptions of Candidates." In *Psychological Process*, edited by F. Biocca. Hillsdale, NJ: Lawrence Erlbaum, 1991.

Baukus, R., J.G. Payne, and M. Reisler. "Negative Polispots: Mediated Argument in the Political Arena." In *Argument and Social Practice: Proceedings of the Fourth Sca/Afa Conference on Argumentation*, edited by J.R. Cox, M.O. Sillars and G.B. Walker, 236-52. Annandale, VA: Speech Communication Association, 1985.

Benoit, W.L., J.P. McHale, G.J. Hansen, P.M. Pier, and J.P. McGuire. *Campaign 2000: A Functional Analysis of Presidential Campaign Discourse*. Lanham, MD: Rowman & Littlefield, 2003.

Berko, R.M., A.D. Wolvin, and D.R. Wolvin. *Communicating: A Social and Career Focus*. 9th ed. Boston: Houghton Mifflin Company, 2004.

Bluestone, Barry, and Chait, Jonathan. "Conversation: Clinton's Bequest Reconsidered." *American Prospect*, 11, no. 4 (2000): 18–25.

Brummett, B. "Towards a Theory of Silence as a Political Strategy." *Quarterly Journal of Speech* 66 (1980): 289–303.

Chang, W.H., J.J. Park, and S.W. Shim. "Effectiveness of Negative Political Advertising." *Web Journal of Mass Communication Research* 2, no. 1 (1998).

Corsi, J.R. *The Obama Nation: Leftist Politics and the Cult of Personality*. New York: Simon & Schuster, 2008.

Dymond, J. "Who Runs the Bush White House?" Review of Reviewed Item. BBC News, (2001), http://news.bbc.co.uk/1/hi/world/americas/1304014.stm.

Elias, M., and J. Sandler. 2004. "Re: Swift Boat Veterans for Truth." gwu.edu/%7Eaction/2004/ads04/dem080504ltrswift.html (accessed May 26, 2008).

Garramone, G.M. "Voter Responses to Negative Political Ads." *Journalism Quarterly* 61, no. 2 (1984): 250–59.

Garramone, G.M., C.K. Atkin, B.E. Pinkleton, and R.T. Cole. "Effects of Negative Political Advertising on the Political Process." *Journal of Broadcasting & Electronic Media* 34, no. 3 (1990): 299–311.

Goodman, W. "The Airwaves: A Few Ideas for the Next Election." Review of Reviewed Item. *New York Times*, (1996), nyu.edu/gsas/dept/politics/seminars/russian5.pdf.

Green, J. "Karl Rove in a Corner." *Atlantic Monthly* 2004.

Halper, J. "Dirty Politics." In *Flashpoint*: KPFA, 2006.

Herbert, G. 2004. "Campaign Finance Groups File Fec Complaint Charging 'Swift Boat Veterans for Truth' Is Violating Federal Campaign Finance Laws." www.gwu.edu/%7Eaction/2004/ads04/sbvtcomplaint.html. (accessed May 27, 2008).

Jamieson, J.H. *Packaging the Presidency: A History and Criticism of Presidential Campaign Advertising*. 2nd ed. New York: Oxford University Press, 1992.

Johnson-Cartee, K.S., and G. Copeland. *Combating Negative Advertising: Proactive and Reactive Strategies*. Westport, CT: Praeger, 1997.

———. *Negative Political Advertising: Coming of Age*. Mahwah, NJ: Lawrence Erlbaum, 1991.

Kern, M. *Thirty-Second Politics: Political Advertising in the Eighties*. New York: Praeger, 1989.

Kerry-Edwards 2004 Campaign Ads. n.d. www.cbsnews.com/elements/2004/03/04/in_depth_politics/videoarchive603962_0_2_page.shtml (accessed June 13, 2008).

Luo, M. "Ready to Attack Obama, If Some Money Arrives." Review of Reviewed Item. *New York Times*, (2008), www.nytimes.com/2008/06/21/us/politics/21ads.html?hp=&pagewanted=all.

McCroskey, James. "A summary of Experimental Research on the Effects of Evidence in Persuasive Communication. *Quarterly Journal of Speech*, 55 (1969): 169-76.

———. The Effects of Evidence as an Inhibitor of Counter-Persuasion. *Speech Monographs*, 37, no. 3 (1970): 188–93.

McGuire, W.J. "Inducing Resistance to Persuasion: Some Contemporary Approaches." In *Advances in Experimental Social Psychology*, edited by L. Berkowitz, 191–229. New York: Academic, 1964.

Meister, R. "What Is to Be Done? Thinking Politically about the 2004 Election." *Theory & Event* 8, no. 2 (2005).

Moore, J., and W. Slater. *Bush's Brain: How Karl Rove Made George W. Bush Presidential*. Hoboken, NJ: John Wiley and Sons, 2004.

Mosk, M. "An Attack That Came Out of the Ether: Scholar Looks for First Link in E-Mail Chain about Obama." Review of Reviewed Item. *Washington Post*, (2008), www.washingtonpost.com/wpdyn/content/article/2008/06/27/AR2008062703781.html?sid=ST2008062703939&pos=.

Multiple. 2004. "Swift Veterans Letter to John Kerry." http://horse.he.net/~swiftpow/article.php?story=20040629220813790 (accessed May 21, 2008).

Mutz, D.C., P.M. Sniderman, and R.A. Brody. *Political Persuasion and Attitude Change.* Ann Arbor, MI: University of Michigan Press, 1996.

O'Neill, J.E., and J.L. Corsi. 2004. Advantage Swift Vets. www.combatvetsagainstkerry.com/unfit_epilogue.pdf (accessed May 24, 2008).

Overby, P. "Political Ads from '527' Groups Get Cold Shoulder." Review of Reviewed Item. *NPR,* (2008), www.npr.org/templates/story/story.php?storyId=90907225.

Pfau, M., and M. Burgoon. "Inoculation in Political Campaign Communication." *Human Communication Research* 15 (1988): 91–111.

Pfau, M., H.C. Kenski, M. Nitz, and J. Sorenson. "Efficacy of Inoculation Strategies in Promoting Resistance to Political Attack Messages: Application to Direct Mail." *Communication Monographs* 57 (1990): 1–12.

Pfau, M., D. Park, R.L. Holbert, and J. Cho. "The Effects of Party- and Pac-Sponsored Issue Advertising and the Potential of Inoculation to Combat Its Impact on the Democratic Process." *American Behavioral Scientist* 44 (2001): 2379–97.

Rich, Frank. "How Kerry Became a Girly-Man." *New York Times,* September 5, 2004.

Rosen, M. "Story Is None Too 'Swift'." Review of Reviewed Item. *Rocky Mountain News,* (2006), www.rockymountainnews.com/drmn/opinion_columnists/article/0,2777,DRMN_23972_5096616,00.html.

Sabato, L. *The Rise of Political Consultants: New Way of Winning Elections.* New York: Basic Books, 1981.

Salmore, Barbara G., and Stephen A. Salmore. *Candidates, Parties, and Campaigns: Electoral Politics in America.* Washington, DC: CQ Press, 1985.

"Swift Boat Vets and POWS for Truth '527' Political Organization Filing Information." (n.d.).

"Swift Liars: Kerry-Edwards Campaign Response." n.d. www.democraticunderground.com/discuss/duboard.php?az=view_oet&address=358x2555. (accessed May 23, 2008).

Tinkham, S.F., and R.A. Weaver-Lariscy. "A Diagnostic Approach to Assessing the Impact of Negative Political Television Commercials." *Journal of Broadcasting & Electronic Media* 37 (1993): 377–99.

Zernike, K. "Veterans Long to Reclaim the Name 'Swift Boat'." Review of Reviewed Item. *New York Times,* (2008), www.nytimes.com/2008/06/30/us/politics/30swift.html?_r=1&oref=slogin.

# 8

# The Possible Future of 527s

*Melissa M. Smith*

Politics is a game that requires money. Stemming the flow of that money—or at least regulating who can give it, who can take it, and how it can be used—is part of the campaign reform shell game. As new reforms are discussed, individuals and organizations are already looking for potential loopholes that can be exploited. It was no different when the Bipartisan Campaign Finance Reform Act (also known as McCain-Feingold) was signed into law in 2002. Because of the new law, individuals who wanted to donate large amounts of money to federal elections could no longer give large sums of unregulated money to the national parties. Instead, many of these large donors began funneling their money into non-profit groups commonly known as 527 organizations. Rather than stem the flow of "soft money," donors simply found another outlet for their money and influence.

These 527 organizations had a major impact on the 2004 presidential election. Some observers credit the ads run by the Swift Boat Veterans for Truth with overwhelming Sen. John Kerry just after the Democratic primary, when he had few financial resources. The organization not only produced television ads, but it also published a book and represented its views on television and radio talk shows.[1] The wounds these messages inflicted on Kerry's campaign proved difficult to overcome, as they created doubts about his credibility and leadership. Although millions of dollars were spent on Kerry's behalf by 527s,[2] their messages seemed to lack the impact of the well-timed Swift Boat ads, and they were many times off-target when compared to Kerry's own campaign messages.

After the 2004 election, critics of 527 organizations asked for greater regulation of the groups. Although the FEC put new regulations into place, many of those changes have now been reversed. This chapter looks at recent and possible future campaign reform involving 527s and the impact that such reforms could have on future political campaigns.

## FLUID ORGANIZATIONS

The 527 organizations have the ability to spring up quickly, make an impact on an election, and then become inactive or disband. Because they often haven't been forced to register as a political committee with the FEC, the groups have fewer contribution and expenditure reports, so their activities are more difficult to track. While this can offer significant political advantages for those making use of a 527, it creates a bit of a regulation challenge for the Federal Election Commission. When the FEC receives a complaint about an organization, the investigation into the allegations could take several months; by then, a 527 group could have disbanded. This means that penalties assessed against 527 groups generally come *after* an election, leaving them time to have an effect on proposed legislation or a political race. This causes critics of 527s to assert that they should automatically be forced to register as political committees so that they can be under greater scrutiny during an election.

Current commission guidelines require that organizations file paperwork to become a regulated political committee if 1) the organization meets the FEC definition of "express advocacy" or contribution regulations and 2) if it is judged to have as its major purpose federal campaign activity. Thus, if an organization specifically endorses or opposes a particular candidate, it is most likely engaging in "express advocacy" according to FEC guidelines. If most of its money is spent on influencing federal elections, it can be judged to have as its main purpose federal campaign activity. Most of the time, though, this doesn't become apparent until after an election. For instance, Progress For America Voter Fund was very active in the 2004 presidential election, raising almost $45 million in contributions.[3] After the election, the FEC determined that $41 million of those funds came from "excessive contributions from individuals" and another $2 million was donated by "sources prohibited from making contributions" under the Federal Election Campaign Act.[4] Basically, the FEC said that the group was functioning like a regulated political committee although it had not registered as such. The organization was fined $750,000, the third-largest penalty in the FEC's history.

However, the fine came three years after the election was over, rendering the penalty useless in terms of the outcome of the 2004 election. The organization admitted to no wrongdoing, as did none of the four 527s that were fined by the FEC following the election. Although the same basic rules are still in place for 527s, the FEC said these fines show that it is serious about cracking down on organizations that do not properly register as federal political committees.

To comply with FEC regulation and avoid having to register as a political committee (which would bring much more regulation and oversight), many organizations have begun to do two things: 1) more carefully design messages to avoid express advocacy, and 2) spend money through other organizations that are less obvious FEC targets. For instance, many groups are now donating money to 501c(4) groups, which are considered social welfare groups. This simply means that this type of organization can do the same things as 527s, except it must be done as a "secondary activity."[5] Another advantage is that some 501c(4) groups—the ones that do not take corporate or union donations and have no shareholders or business income—are exempt from the ban on corporate spending for express advocacy. So, these types of groups "can urge voters to vote for or against candidates and even do so during periods shortly before elections when 501c(4) corporate spending on electioneering ads (broadcast ads mentioning a candidate) were banned" by the provisions of BCRA.[6] Many interest groups have established 501c(4) groups, including such well-known lobbying interests as the National Rifle Association, Defenders of Wildlife Action Fund, the League of Conservation Voters and Planned Parenthood Action Fund. Of course, these groups also have PACs, so they can use different organizations for different purposes.

Some political organizations that were active in the 2004 election, such as MoveOn Voter Fund, have terminated their 527 groups. MoveOn disbanded its 527 during the 2008 election, crediting this move to then-Sen. Barack Obama, who was critical of 527 groups. Instead, MoveOn relied on its PAC, which can only accept donations of up to $5,000 per individual.[7]

Overall, 527s had less impact on the 2008 election than the one in 2004. More than $180 million was spent by 527s, with most of this money being spent to support Democratic candidates.[8] While this is no small figure, it does pale somewhat in comparison to the $338 million spent by 527 groups during the 2004 election. It is clear that fewer organizations made use of 527s in 2008, and that could be a trend that continues in the 2010 elections unless changes are made regarding the point at which 527s are required to register as political committees.

## Congressional Action

Following the 2004 presidential election, there were calls for Congress to take action to place more regulations on 527 organizations. Sen. Russ Feingold (D-WI) and Sen. John McCain (R-AZ) are two of the most visible proponents of additional regulation of 527s. Together they introduced the 527 Reform Act in the Senate in 2006. A similar version of this bill, sponsored by Rep. Christopher Shays (R-CT), passed the House on April 5, 2006. The Senate bill was read twice, but then faded away.

The bill would have required 527s to register as federal political committees and therefore be subject to the same contribution limits that apply to other groups seeking to influence federal elections. Individual donations to 527s would have been restricted to $25,000 or less. Feingold said the current system gives an unfair advantage to this type of organization. "By allowing 527s to funnel massive contributions from wealthy interests into federal elections, the FEC has undermined the campaign finance system."[9] Feingold refers to these organizations as "the 527 loophole," and has said that he wants to work for change so that the country has "a campaign finance system that restores our citizenry's faith in the electoral process and in their elected officials."[10]

But apparently not as many senators and members of the House are as concerned about this problem as Feingold. The likelihood that any significant change regarding 527s will come from Congress seems very slight. There are simply too many other large issues for Congress to tackle, and there is no pressing reason for this legislation to become a high priority.

There simply doesn't seem to be the political will or urgency to take up these reforms. "I don't think anyone sees campaign reform as a national priority. Campaign reform happens either after a scandal or when everything is going along fairly well and the Congress can take up those issues."[11] For these reasons, few people expect any new regulation regarding 527s to come from Congress in the upcoming sessions.

## Emily's List v. FEC

In October 2009, a three-judge panel of the U.S. Court of Appeals for the D.C. Circuit handed down a ruling that has the potential to significantly change non-profit political committee involvement in elections. After the massive amounts of money poured into 527s by wealthy individuals in the 2004 election, the FEC instituted new rules in 2005, capping individual contributions to non-profit groups to $5,000 a year and requiring that non-profits pay for a large percentage of election-related activities out of their "hard-money" accounts. Because of these restrictions, non-profit groups were limited in what they could spend for election-related activities such as advertisements, get-out-the-vote efforts, and voter registration activities.

The regulations also required that donations to non-profits be considered "hard money" if a corresponding solicitation indicated that donations would be used to support the election or defeat of a federal candidate.[12] An example of this might be if "X" organization sent an e-mail message to supporters or members urging that they donate money to help it air TV ads opposing Sen. Harry Reid (D-NV). Because of the rules changes that went into effect in 2005, any money raised in response to this solicitation would have been deemed "hard money," and subject to a $5,000 cap on individual donations.

Emily's List is a political action committee that works to elect female Democratic candidates who support abortion rights. The group has both federal and non-federal accounts and works for Democratic candidates in state elections, as well as in federal elections. The group decided to bring a case against the FEC, arguing against these new restrictions on hard-money contributions for political activities. Emily's List argued that the FEC exceeded its authority by placing limits on how organizations could spend money for non-federal activities or elections. It also argued that the restrictions violated the organization's First Amendment rights by putting in place unconstitutionally vague and overbroad regulations regarding contributions and expenditures.[13]

The appeals court supported the arguments made by Emily's List, saying the new FEC rules worked to limit the free speech rights of non-profit political groups. The appeals court ruling effectively nullified the cap on individual contributions, stating that "the First Amendment, as interpreted by the Supreme Court, protects the right of individual citizens to spend unlimited amounts to express their views about policy issues and candidates for public office."[14] The opinion also stated that citizens have the right to band together and pool their resources as an unincorporated group or a non-profit organization. The ruling affects non-party political groups including some PACs and 501c organizations, as well as 527 groups.

## Implications for 2010

This ruling could have at least two major implications for upcoming elections. First, it will allow non-party groups to raise what would have previously been termed "soft money" that can be used to influence federal elections. Without caps on donor contributions, organizations will be able to raise and spend money with few restrictions. These non-party organizations "are now free to accept unlimited contributions, to spend unlimited funds independently supporting or opposing federal candidates."[15] Some argue this could lead to a situation more reminiscent of the 2004 election, in which 527s were quite visible in their support or opposition of presidential candidates. "One of the things we know about outside groups, as opposed to political parties, is that they run more negative ads . . . This could lead to a more negative campaign season."[16]

The ruling will also allow groups to raise soft money by telling donors they are specifically targeting a particular candidate. For instance, if a 527 organization targets a particular candidate in a federal election, the organization is now free to send out a solicitation for donations indicating the funds will be used to target that particular candidate. Before, any donations received in response to this type of solicitation were deemed "hard money" and subject to the $5,000 cap. Now that the cap has been removed, 527s have the opportunity to raise more money for upcoming elections.

Some argue this returns 527s to having an advantage over national political parties. "The ruling will provide a boost to outside groups at the expense of established political parties, which must continue to function under stringent financial limits."[17] These limits were put in place by BCRA when it was signed into law in 2002.

The FEC chose not to appeal the court's ruling, and on December 17, 2009, it approved steps to bring the agency's regulations into compliance with the court's opinion. This will allow 527s to operate under the looser restrictions as early as the mid-term elections in 2010. Some observers say this is helpful, as it clears the way for organizations to have a greater understanding of the rules as they head into another election season. "It is important for groups planning to participate in the political process to have certainty going into 2010, and the [FEC] is helping provide that by not appealing the court's decision."[18]

This ruling could pave the way for more 527 activity in upcoming elections, but the FEC is still looking closely at the activities of 527 organizations. As noted earlier, though, penalties regarding campaign election activity are usually assessed following an election, leaving the groups relatively free from scrutiny during a particular campaign.

## OTHER PENDING COURT CASES

Two other court cases are working their way through the federal system that could have a direct impact on future elections, and one of them specifically relates to 527s and current rules regarding political committee registration. Under current regulations, a group must register as a political committee with the FEC when it raises or spends more than $1,000 in a calendar year. Registration with the FEC places the organization under the FEC's regulations regarding a group's contributions and expenditures.

*SpeechNow.org v. FEC* is a challenge to the FEC's restrictions on independent campaign spending and its rules forcing groups to register as political committees. SpeechNow.org is a non-profit, unincorporated association organized as a 527 group. The group contends that forcing it to register as a political committee restricts its association guaranteed under the First Amendment and will limit the financial amount that an individual may contribute to the organization. SpeechNow and the other plaintiffs argue that the regulations unconstitutionally restrict an individuals' freedom of speech by limiting the amount that an individual can contribute to the organization. This works to restrict the amount the organization may spend, because its donations are limited. SpeechNow also argues that the reporting required of political committees is unconstitutionally burdensome.[19] Oral arguments in the case were set for January 2010 in the D.C. Circuit Court of Appeals. Supporters of SpeechNow's argument point to *Emily's List v. FEC* as a sign that the federal courts may be sympathetic to their arguments.

Another case that could have a direct bearing on future elections is *Republican National Committee v. FEC*. This case challenges the constitutionality of the ban on soft money put in place by McCain-Feingold, and it also challenges the limits on how much parties may spend in coordination with a candidate's official campaign. A group of national and state Republican Party committees contend that the soft money ban put in place by BCRA is unconstitutional because it prohibits the national party from raising and spending soft money for influencing state elections, for redistricting, for grassroots lobbying, for various types of litigation, for voter registration, for get-out-the-vote drives and for funding public communications that promote or attack federal candidates. The case does not challenge soft-money regulations put in place for "unambiguous" campaign activities related to a federal candidate.[20] The case is currently before the U.S. District Court in the District of Columbia.

While the RNC case may not have a direct bearing on 527 organizations, the lifting of soft money restrictions to political parties could causes a decrease in funds making their ways to 527 groups in future elections.

## CONCLUSIONS

There are at least three different sources for campaign finance reform: Congress, the FEC, and the courts. Of these three, the major revisions seem to be coming from cases working their way through the federal court system. Congress seems unwilling to tackle 527 campaign reforms, even though a handful of elected officials continue to work toward that goal. The FEC has attempted to impose greater restrictions on 527s, but many of its efforts have been reversed by the federal courts, which have equated individual financial donations and non-profit group expenditures with free speech. "I think the FEC would like to make 527 reforms, but the Supreme Court has ruled numerous times against reforms that limit First Amendment rights."[21]

This echoes earlier decisions by the U.S. Supreme Court, including *Buckley v. Valeo* in 1974, in which the high court found that the limits that had been placed on expenditures by individuals or groups for a specific candidate, on overall campaign expenditures, and on those by an individual candidate from personal funds were unconstitutional.[22] The ruling effectively removed the ceiling on what could be *spent* by those running for federal office. The majority opinion stated that limits on what could be spent by individuals, groups or candidates "place substantial and direct restrictions on the ability of candidates, citizens, and associations to engage in protected political expression."[23] This ruling is widely seen as opening the door for so-called soft money by establishing that political ads not sponsored by a candidate and which do not expressly endorse a particular candidate are not subject to contribution limits or disclosure requirements.[24]

Thirty years later, the courts still seem reluctant to impose limits on expenditures, and now have also loosened the restrictions on what can be given by individuals to non-profit groups. Some restrictions, such as the amounts individuals can donate directly to campaigns or political parties, are still in place, but donations to non-profit groups or money spent by individuals on behalf of a candidate are now subject to fewer regulations and limits.

What seems to be happening is a trend toward deregulation of non-party political groups. While the Emily's List case was a victory for donations to non-profit political groups, it doesn't address the flip side of the case for 527s, which is that they still have to register as political committees if they raise more than $1,000 a year. This, they contend, places them under too much FEC regulation. Critics challenge that assertion, noting that the lack of regulation of 527s puts those types of organizations at an advantage in both fundraising and expenditures. That part of the 527 puzzle will probably be addressed through the SpeechNow.org case, and observers are watching that case closely.

What does this mean for the future of 527s? It seems that major provisions of BCRA are slowly being dismantled by the federal courts. As always happens, court cases take a long time to wind through the court system, and some of them never make it beyond the appeals stage. But a few significant ones, such as *Emily's List v. FEC* and *SpeechNow.org v. FEC* have the potential to influence 527s for many years to come.

The most likely scenario is that non-party, non-profit groups will increase their profiles in the 2010 and 2012 elections. A former FEC general counsel predicts that "the role of outside political groups can be expected to 'expand dramatically as soon as 2010.'"[25] That means more fundraising and expenditures by independent groups, which increases the likelihood of more controversy and more calls for regulation.

## NOTES

1. Kate Zernike and Jim Rutenberg, "The Birth of an Anti-Kerry Ad," *New York Times*, 20 Aug. 2004, www.nytimes.com/2004/08/20/politics/campaign/20swift.html (21 Dec. 2009).
2. Michael Janofsky, "Advocacy Groups Spent Record Amount on 2004 Election," *New York Times*, 17 Dec. 2004, query.nytimes.com/gst/fullpage.html?res=9E04E0D71430F934A25751C1A9629C8B63 (21 Dec. 2009).
3. FEC release, "FEC to Collect $750,000 Civil Penalty from Progress for America Voter Fund," 28 Feb. 2007, http://www.fec.gov/press/press2007/20070228MUR.html (21 Dec. 2009)
4. FEC release, "FEC to Collect."
5. Steve Weissman, "Fast Start for Soft Money Groups in 2008 Election," 3 April 2008, http://www.cfinst.org/pr/prRelease.aspx?ReleaseID=188 (22 Dec. 2009)
6. Weissman, "Fast Start."
7. Jayson K. Jones & Ana C. Rosado, "MoveOn Terminates Its 527," *New York Times* Caucus Blog, 20 June 2008, thecaucus.blogs.nytimes.com/2008/06/20/moveon-terminates-its-527/ (22 Dec. 2009).
8. Blake Dvorak, "An Interesting Factoid about Election 2008," Real Clear Politics, 4 Nov. 2008, www.realclearpolitics.blogs.time.com/page/128/?xid=rss-blogs (3 Dec. 2009).
9. Sen. Russ Feingold, "Issues, Campaign Finance Reform, 527s," feingold.senate.gov/issues_cfr_527.html (20 Dec. 2009).
10. Russ Feingold, "Campaign Finance Reform Returning Government to the People," www.russfeingold.org/issues/campaign-finance-reform.html (20 Dec. 2009)
11. Jim Kitchens, e-mail message to author, 17 Dec. 2009
12. Federal Election Commission, Legal Opinion, 18 Sept. 2009, www.fec.gov/law/litigation/emilyslist_08_ac_opinion.pdf (22 Dec. 2009).
13. Federal Election Commission, Legal Opinion.
14. Federal Election Commission, Legal Opinion.
15. Del Quentin Wilber & Dan Eggen, "Federal Appeals Court Voids Campaign Finance Reform Rules," 19 Sept. 2009, http://www.washingtonpost.com/wpdyn/content/article/2009/09/18/AR2009091801698.html (27 Dec. 2009).
16. Wilber and Eggen, "Federal Appeals Court."
17. Wilber and Eggen, "Federal Appeals Court."
18. OMB Watch, "FEC Decides Not to Appeal EMILY'S List Decision," 28 Oct. 2009, www.ombwatch.org/node/10512 (21 Dec. 2009)
19. Federal Election Commission, Ongoing Litigation, www.fec.gov/law/litigation/speechnow.shtml (28 Dec. 2009).
20. Federal Election Commission, Ongoing Litigation, www.fec.gov/law/litigation/rnc_08.shtml (28 Dec. 2009).
21. Kitchens, e-mail message.
22. *Buckley v. Valeo*, (424 U.S. 1), 1976, supreme.justia.com/us/424/1/case.html (27 Dec. 2009).
23. *Buckley v. Valeo*, 1976

24. Ryan M. Ellis, "Electioneering Communication under the Bipartisan Campaign Reform Act of 2002," *Case Western Reserve Law Review*, no. 54, 187–224. Joseph E. Cantor, "Campaign Financing in Federal Elections: A Guide to the Law and its Operation," in *Campaign financing in the United States issues and laws*, ed. Auguste V. Anschutz (New York: Nova Science Publishers, Inc.), 55-105.

25. Eliza Newlin Carney, "Opponents of Campaign Finance Rules Are Moving on Multiple Fronts," 26 Oct. 2009, Campaign Legal Center, http://www.campaignlegalcenter.org/press-3760.html (28 Dec. 2009).

## BIBLIOGRAPHY (PARTIAL LIST)


Carney, Eliza Newlin. "Opponents of Campaign Finance rules are Moving on Multiple Fronts," 26 Oct. 2009, Campaign Legal Center, www.campaignlegalcenter.org/press-3760.html (28 Dec. 2009).

Ellis, Ryan M. "Electioneering Communication Under the Bipartisan Campaign Reform Act of 2002," *Case Western Reserve Law Review*, no. 54, 187–224.

Federal Election Commission Release, "FEC to Collect $750,000 Civil Penalty from Progress For America Voter Fund," 28 Feb. 2007, www.fec.gov/press/press2007/20070228MUR.html (21 Dec. 2009)

Federal Election Commission, Ongoing Litigation, www.fec.gov/law/litigation/speechnow.shtml (28 Dec. 2009).

Janofsky, Michael. "Advocacy Groups Spent Record Amount on 2004 Election," *New York Times*, 17 Dec. 2004, query.nytimes.com/gst/fullpage.html?res=9E04E0D71430F934A25751C1A9629C8B63 (21 Dec. 2009).

OMB Watch, "FEC Decides Not to Appeal EMILY'S List Decision," 28 Oct. 2009, www.ombwatch.org/node/10512 (21 Dec. 2009)

Wilber, Del Quintin & Dan Eggen, "Federal Appeals Court Voids Campaign Finance Reform Rules," 19 Sept. 2009, www.washingtonpost.com/wpdyn/content/article/2009/09/18/AR2009091801698.html (27 Dec. 2009).

# 9

# The Future of Campaign Finance Laws

*Melissa M. Smith*

Money is the fuel for political campaign messages—an essential and necessary ingredient. For their campaigns to be successful, candidates must have enough money to communicate their ideas.

No wonder, then, that politicians and their campaigns scour the campaign election laws, looking for loopholes and ways to use the system to their political advantage. As the laws change, the campaigns find new ways to circumvent the system and keep funds flowing into their campaign coffers.

Campaign finance laws often directly impact the campaign and its messages. These rules can determine who can give money and how much can be given, and they can even outline how and when money can be spent by political campaigns or independent organizations supporting a particular candidate. They prohibit coordination of messages between campaigns and independent organizations, and even prescribe the specific uses of money given to state political parties.

Some potential candidates—and even those already holding elective office—hate fundraising, and that becomes a factor in whether or not they run. Former Illinois Senator Paul Simon retired from politics, citing his dislike for the daily necessity of raising money.[1] It is common for members of the Senate to raise \$5,000 a week for six years, and Simon said he had wearied of the money chase. A study in 2000 found that 43 percent of those running for Congress spent one-fourth of their time raising money. Nearly one of every five reported spending almost half their time raising money.[2] It's reasonable to expect that those numbers have increased, as the amount of money needed to win a federal office has continued to increase.

The discussion about campaign finance reform—and its possible planned and unplanned consequences—is ongoing in Washington, the federal courts, and even in some state legislatures. That discussion often leads to proposed legislation, yet rarely results in new law, partially because it is difficult to get lawmakers to agree on how to change the existing rules. Portions of the Bipartisan Campaign Finance Reform of 2002 are still making their way through the federal circuit and appeals courts, as well as the United States Supreme Court, and these rulings could have substantial impact on future federal political campaigns. This chapter will look at possible future Congressional reform, as well as cases under review by the U.S. Supreme Court. It will also include the predictions of communication scholars and political consultants regarding the future of campaign finance reform.

## MONEY AND LEGITIMACY

Campaign finance laws limit fundraising, or at least make it harder than many campaigns would prefer. Campaign consultants and workers often end up fighting over those scarce resources. That's why Franzen[3] noted that "many of the difficulties that arise between consultants and their clients revolve around money."[4]

Further, perhaps the most overlooked role of campaign finance laws in campaigns is the rhetorical impact that money has on campaigns—an element that has been described as "the rhetoric of money."[5] The amount of money raised by the campaign becomes a scorecard that opponents and the media use to judge the early success of a campaign. Thus, as Powell and Cowart noted, "Early [fundraising] success draws media attention to the campaign, bestows legitimacy to the campaign efforts, and puts pressure on the competition."[6] Steen noted that the reporting of campaign fundraising often becomes a "self-fulfilling prophecy" that drives out competitors and discourages others from entering the contest.[7] One observer, Larry Markinson of the Center for Responsive Politics, noted that during the 2000 Republican primary season, George W. Bush became a shoo-in for the nomination by July 1999 because of his extensive fundraising. "The funders have decided who the next nominee is going to be six months before anyone casts a vote," he complained.[8]

Markinson's complaint is understandable, but it also ignores a basic fact of modern political campaigns. Money is not only the fuel of the campaign, but it also contributes to the legitimacy of a political candidate. As Powell and Cowert noted, "money buys the means of political speech."[9] Without money, a campaign cannot effectively distribute its messages, and that means that a candidate will not appear legitimate in the eyes of the mass media, which is vitally important. Candidates seen as legitimate receive news coverage. Those not seen as legitimate are often overlooked when it comes to news coverage. Thus, the race to raise money has at least two purposes: fund the dissemination of campaign messages and increase legitimacy in the eyes the mass media.

This is why the debate over campaign finance reform is so important. For some candidates, the lack of access to funds has the possibility of limiting the campaign's effectiveness or ending a campaign prematurely. This fuels the call for an "equalization" of the campaign process, and a challenger would generally benefit more from these changes than an incumbent. The realization that campaign laws are written by those already in office is not lost on most observers. Those already serving in Congress would like to retain their seats, so they are unlikely to craft legislation that would endanger their own political survival.

Even when new legislation is enacted, the results are often almost negligible. Although the Bipartisan Campaign Reform Act was signed into law in 2002, the following two presidential elections saw more money flowing into campaigns than ever before, despite the new restrictions. The 2008 election went down in the record books as the election with the most money ever raised by a presidential candidate, along with substantial amounts spent by political parties and independent organizations. Consultant John Rowley says campaign finance reform is "sometimes like squeezing Jell-O in your hand . . . it oozes somewhere."[10] Rowley says "campaign finance reform usually has mixed results because you cannot get the influence of money out of politics."[11]

But some members of Congress continue to try to reform the system, introducing legislation almost every session aimed at lowering the amount of money that candidates need to raise for political races.

## Fair Elections Now

One piece of legislation under consideration in fall 2009 was the Fair Elections Now Act, which would provide for public financing of congressional campaigns.[12] The bill, which was first introduced in Congress in 2007, is supported by several lawmakers, including John Larson (C-CT), chairman of the House Democratic Caucus and Sen. Arlen Specter (D-PA). As of fall 2009, there were more than 100 co-sponsors in the House. Larson describes the current system as "completely legal and lawful, but corrosive," and says it is in need of reform so that both elected and prospective members of Congress don't have to spend so much time raising money. [13]

The legislation calls for combining small donations (no more than $100 each) with matching public funds. Candidates who can show a broad base of support through small donations would have the option of receiving public matching funds. A caveat is that, if a candidate accepts the public funds, he or she must forego large contributions from special-interest groups. To qualify, candidates for the House would have to collect 1,500 contributions from people in their states and raise a total of $50,000. The proposed rules for a Senate candidate would be different, mainly because states vary in population. A Senate candidate would be required to raise a set amount of small contributions amounting to 10 percent of the primary Fair Elections funding.[14]

Additionally, participating candidates would receive a 20 percent reduction from the lowest broadcast rates and could be eligible for additional matching Federal Elections funds if they are facing a well-financed or self-financed opponent. However, joint fundraising committees between candidates and parties would be prohibited.

As of fall 2009, the Senate bill was still in committee, and it seemed to lack sufficient support to make it to a Senate floor vote. However, the continued activity surrounding the bill indicates that the mood in Congress might be swinging in the direction of supporting public campaign financing.

## STATE-LEVEL REFORM EFFORTS

This seems to be the direction in which many states are also moving. Illinois, Wisconsin, and New York are all considering legislation that would either establish or tighten the rules regarding public financing of campaigns. The motivation given in most cases is that it will allow for a more even playing field, and thus enable more fair elections. For instance, Illinois is one of only six states without any restrictions on financial contributions to candidates. However, the arrest and impeachment of former Gov. Rob Blagojevich, who was accused of attempting to sell President Barack Obama's former Senate seat to the highest bidder, prompted a campaign-finance reform bill that passed the state legislature, but was vetoed by Lt. Gov. Patrick Quinn. Quinn, who replaced Blagojevich, said the bill did not create meaningful reform. So, legislators went back to the drawing board and in October 2009 another campaign reform bill was put forth by the Illinois Speaker of the House. It passed the House Executive Committee on a party-line vote, and it is unclear if the bill has enough support to pass a full House vote.[15]

Substantial reform at the state level is unlikely, but issues regarding corporate contributions, union contributions, and contributions limits could provide the best targets for reformers.[16] This could be the case in California. Various proposals have come before the state legislature for several years, and so far few of them have garnered enough support to make it through the legislature. However, the state is in the forefront of what is called "Clean Elections" public financing. This type of public financing replaces candidate-raised funds almost entirely with public funds. The California Fair Elections Act was signed into law in 2008, and it provides for a public financing pilot project involving candidates for the office of Secretary of State. This measure will be placed on the state's 2010 ballot as a legislatively referred state statute and, if approved, would provide for voluntary full public financing for Secretary of State candidates in 2014 and 2018. This is seen as a test run for future public financing of campaigns and is modeled on similar programs in Arizona and Maine. Currently half of the states offer some type of program that provides state funds to political candidates.

Some people might question this approach, given President Obama's refusal of public financing in his presidential campaign. He was phenomenally successful at fundraising, and he raised much more money through his campaign than he could have obtained through public campaign financing. In fact, Sen. John McCain was often at a disadvantage because he did elect to accept public campaign financing, and he ended up with less money for his campaign needs than Obama. But what worked for Obama won't necessarily transfer well to other candidates, especially those in small races. Obama has pledged to reform the presidential public finance system, but, given the number of other large issues garnering his attention, public financing of elections doesn't seem to have gained a high priority in his administration. However, grass roots activists have been working in several states to push for clean election legislation, and their efforts appear to be gaining traction in several states. It is unclear whether these efforts will gain enough supporters at the congressional level to impact federal campaign finance reform.

Consultant John Rowley sees this going the other way. "Reform usually only follows a scandal and sometimes not even then. Some places are rolling back reforms, like Tennessee. I don't see a trend toward more reform."[17] Rowley added that campaign finance reform doesn't usually poll well with the public, either. Because voters think politicians in general are corrupt, they don't usually believe it when an elected official pushes progressive reforms. Voters don't usually reward politicians for pushing for campaign reform, Rowley said.[18] One example of that could be Sen. John McCain, who was unpopular with many in the Republican Party for helping push BCRA through the Senate. Eight years later, some Republican voters still express distrust of McCain because of his support for this bill.

It seems unlikely that many members of Congress—especially Republicans—would spend much time working to pass new campaign finance laws if the relative benefits to them are so small.

## CAMPAIGN REFORM AND THE WEB

Another direction in which Congress, the FEC, the courts, and even some states might move is to tighten campaign reform regarding online expenditures and campaign fundraising.

In 2002, the FEC ruled that the Internet was exempted from the regulations set forth in the Bipartisan Campaign Reform Act. However, in 2004, the U.S. District Court for the District of Columbia found in *Shays v. FEC* that the commission's ruling was faulty, and that the Internet could not be exempted. In response, the FEC came up with a new definition of public advertising in relation to the Web, and it includes paid advertising placed on someone else's Web site. However, it does not encompass any other form of Internet communication.[19]

The FEC also added new exceptions to the definition of "contribution" and "expenditure" to exempt individual activity or activities qualifying under a media exemption. The FEC has consistently demonstrated a restrained approach regarding the Internet, and these regulations reflected its commitment to keep the vast majority of Internet communication free from campaign finance regulation. The reasoning for such restraint has been that the Internet provides an easy entry point for individuals who wish to participate in the political process, as opposed to mass-media outlets in which there are higher barriers (such as the cost of producing and airing television advertising).

In 2004, and even more in 2008, the Internet played a significant role in the presidential campaigns. More voters than ever went online to find information about the campaigns, to participate in some way, or received information from friends or campaigns. Given the FEC's definition of public communication, much of these activities were not subject to any sort of regulation.

In 2008 the campaigns developed strategies to further incorporate the Web and new media into their campaigns. Many of these efforts were aimed at raising funds, but much emphasis was also given to developing a sense of community among volunteers and encouraging volunteer involvement in the campaigns. Given the success of the Obama campaign in 2008, future candidates will have to decide how much of their budgets should be dedicated to new media such as social networking, texting, YouTube, and Web sites designed for bottom-up campaign organizations. One strategist suggested that "what we need to do moving forward is look at the breakout of budgets between phones, direct mail and TV, and allocate proportionally based on where the eyeballs are."[20] And the eyeballs are moving online. In the United States, more than half of the entire adult population went online during the 2008 election to take part in or get information about candidates and campaigns. The Internet is now second only to television as a leading source for campaign news, having surpassed newspapers as a source of news in 2008.[21]

This means that future candidates must develop the ability to do two things: find their supporters and then empower them wherever they are. For most candidates, that means pouring more resources into a multi-faceted strategy using the Web and other new media as the centerpiece of a campaign. While locating supporters in cyberspace is not an easy task, empowering them is an even more complicated task, requiring expertise in several areas. Campaigns will find that such expertise costs money, requiring yet more funds to be raised.

Barack Obama's fundraising success—going it alone rather than using public funding—may have ended the days of presidential candidates taking public funds during the general election. While Obama was raising millions, John McCain was burdened by his relative lack of available funds. Opinions are split on this, however, with John Rowley saying public financing has come to an end because other campaigns cannot compete if they opt into the system.[22] Others say that isn't completely accurate. "Public financing with inadequate expenditures is demonstrably dead. What the Obama campaign accomplished with its large finance advantage was widespread 'political' speech."[23] Cowart argues that "any system that limits 'political' speech" will simply not be selected as a viable alternative by presidential campaigns.

One thing that is certain is that large amounts of money will be raised via the Internet in upcoming elections. New FEC regulations regarding bundled contributions (bundlers are individuals who collect many small checks up to the $2,300 cap put in place by BCRA) went into effect in March 2009, requiring greater disclosure of amounts bundled by lobbyists, registrants and the PACs of lobbyists and registrants. Basically, this requires members of Congress to give the names of lobbyists who round up contributions on their behalf. But a study commissioned by the Wall Street Journal found that bundlers aren't just rounding up small change for candidates.

The study found about 200 "mega bundlers" who worked in the 2008 presidential election. Mega-bundlers were defined as individuals who raised up to $70,000 each from individuals by channeling it through joint fundraising committees, which then allocated the money according to BCRA regulations. Many of these donations begin as e-mail messages sent from one person to another. One mega-bundler in Texas raised $285,000 for Obama, and said the process was easy and "didn't take any time at all."[24] The checks came in response to a simple e-mail sent by the bundler.

These joint fundraising accounts can take larger donations because they don't give money directly to candidates. The money goes instead to national and state parties, which then spend it to support the presidential candidates. Although BCRA was designed to limit the influence of large donors on the federal election process, mega-bundlers were very busy in the 2008 election. McCain had 84 mega-bundlers, while Obama had 119, ". . . when you can drive up with a truckload of money to give a candidate, it's hard to see how that's limiting influence."[25]

Interestingly, the Obama campaign highly publicized its success in raising money online from small donors, but did not play up the amounts raised by high-end bundlers. Although there is nothing illegal about using bundlers, it does present an image counter to the one that Obama cultivated during the election, which was of wide grassroots support and small-donor success.

While some have called for further reform of the online fundraising and expenditure process, the FEC has not shown interest in pursuing this topic. The agency requires that online fundraising activities comply with the Internet Communications Act recordkeeping and reporting provisions. These provisions apply to federal political committees, corporations, labor organizations and trade associations.

Congress has also shown a lack of interest in pursuing tighter regulation of online fundraising, perhaps because elected officials sense the fundraising potential for their own upcoming races. Thus, it is unlikely that new rules governing online fundraising will be put in place by either the FEC or Congress.

## COURT CASES AND REFORM

Most campaign finance reform originates either in Congress or with the FEC. However, individuals who feel their rights have been harmed or limited by new laws have the right to pursue redress through the courts. Therefore, the U.S. Supreme Court and the federal court system have long been arbiters in federal campaign finance reform. Since its enaction in 2002, several provisions of the Bipartisan Campaign Reform Act have been challenged in federal courts. In general, BCRA has not fared well in these court cases. Several are still at the federal appeals court level, while others have worked their way through to the Supreme Court.

Some of the larger cases decided by the U.S. Supreme Court involving this legislation were FEC v. Wisconsin Right to Life [26] and Shays v. FEC.[27] The Wisconsin Right to Life case, decided in 2007, was seen as a blow to "electioneering communication" as outlined in BCRA. In its decision, the Supreme Court crafted a major exception to the limitations that were placed by BCRA on broadcast ads within thirty days of a primary or sixty days of a general election. In support of Wisconsin Right to Life, the court said that, unless an ad could not reasonably be interpreted as anything but an ad urging the support of or defeat of a candidate, it would be eligible for what was termed an "as applied" exception to the BCRA limits on issue ads. The court said that in cases such as this one in which there is doubt regarding whether the electioneering test is met, "the First Amendment requires us to err on the side of protecting political speech rather than suppressing it" and "we give the benefit of the doubt to speech, not censorship." This was generally seen as a blow against a major provision of BCRA.[28]

In Shays III v. FEC[29] decided in June 2008, the U.S. Court of Appeals stuck down two revised FEC regulations, including part of one regarding coordinated communication (which was originally struck down in Shays II), one regarding the definition of GOTV and voter registration activity, and a rule allowing federal candidates to solicit soft money at state party fundraisers. The only part upheld by the court was a provision regarding the "firewall safe harbor," which refers to the separation between those working on a candidate's campaign and others working for outside groups making independent expenditures. This was seen as another blow for the FEC, which had attempted to re-write these regulations after they were previously struck down by the high court.

### *Citizens United v. FEC*

A case currently being considered by the U.S. Supreme Court could have far-reaching effects on political campaigns. In *Citizens United v. FEC,*[30] the court was faced with deciding whether an anti-Hillary Clinton documentary produced during the 2008 presidential campaign violated restrictions on corporate spending in federal elections. The documentary was produced by Citizens United, an ideologically based group that takes for-profit corporate funding. The group wanted to air the documentary during the Democratic Party primary through a cable television "video on demand" service and sponsor advertisements for it on television. A cable television operator consortium would have made it available (in exchange for a $1.2 million fee) free "on demand" as part of an Election 2008 series.

The FEC blocked the move, saying it was basically a long political ad promoting the defeat of a specific candidate, and it was produced by an advocacy group that had taken corporate contributions. BCRA bars corporate-funded television broadcasts just before both primaries and elections. The move was challenged by Citizens United, which argued that it limited the constitutional speech of corporations, unions and trade organizations.

Citizens United's president, David Bossie, argued that corporations and unions deserve the same free speech rights as individuals. "We thought it was important on multiple levels, not just our firm. We thought it transcended all of campaign finance."[31] Bossie and his organization felt this case could deal a severe blow to BCRA, legislation that they considered a "great wrong."[32]

The U.S. Supreme Court heard initial arguments in the case in March 2009. However, the Court ordered new arguments for September 2009 after it was unable to reach a decision on whether this documentary violated campaign finance laws.[33]

During the second round of arguments, observers generally felt that the majority of the Justices were supportive of United Citizens' constitutional arguments.[34] Many feel that campaign finance laws are about to change, but are unsure how broad a ruling will be issued by the court. It could rule narrowly and decide that this section of BCRA does not apply to a documentary that is aired through a video-on-demand service. However, it could take a broader approach, which involves a number of possibilities. Any of these broader possibilities opens the door to significant changes in campaign finance law.

Someone who has covered the Supreme Court for fifty-one years predicted that the court will side with Citizens United. But how far it will go is unknown. "In the course of saying for-profit corporations can spend independently, the court could make some very sweeping statements about the free speech rights of organizations that take the corporate form. And they could scuttle a whole lot of restrictions that are at the state level, as well."[35]

As this book was being edited for publication, the Supreme Court issued a ruling on this case. It ruled 5-4 that the government may not ban political spending by corporations in political elections. This could have a wide-ranging effect on future elections, with some campaign finance law experts predicting that it could change the way elections are conducted in this country.[36]

It is certain that this ruling could specifically benefit corporations and unions. Until now, they have been unable to spend money directly. Instead, they provide donations to parties or campaigns. If they were given the opportunity to produce their own political messages, then it could have a direct impact on the political advertising produced and aired during an election. For corporations and unions looking to be involved in upcoming elections, this ruling could offer more possibilities, but also more complications, as the new rules are put into place by the FEC.

For a more comprehensive look at this Supreme Court ruling and its implications, please see the Afterword at the end of this book.

## CONCLUSIONS

It is easy to see why the subject of campaign finance reform has become the province of attorneys. The rules are often complicated, and court cases involving major pieces of legislation generally add more layers to the laws, making it harder for candidates and organizations to both grasp and comply with the rules.

While Congress has traditionally been the source of campaign reform, there seems to be little motivation for reform at this time. Although President Obama vowed to make campaign reform a priority in his administration, he has not devoted much attention to the topic. It is generally felt that, without a major push from Obama or a scandal, no significant campaign finance reform will be forthcoming from Congress in the next few years.

Significant changes could occur in some states, although the legislation is still having a hard time gaining traction in most state legislatures. Grassroots activity could make a difference if it is seen as a long-term process, rather than a short-term lobbying effort in states. Because campaign reform is not a hot-button issue, activists will need to present compelling cases for reform, and that generally means pointing to documented scandals or well-known problems. In some states, this will be difficult to accomplish. In others, such as California or Illinois where reform discussion is ongoing, the odds of reform are much higher.

But the most significant changes in campaign reform will more than likely come from the federal court system, where several elements of BCRA have been challenged. As these court cases work their way through the system, bits and pieces of BCRA are being chipped away or trimmed back. As these changes occur, political candidates, parties, and other organizations are waiting in the wings to see how they will be affected. By the 2012 presidential election several cases, including Citizens United v. FEC, will have worked their way through the system and produced changes in the current laws and regulations.

In the end, LaRaja[37] seems on target when he says that the fight over campaign reform is less a fight over corruption than it is over campaign resources. Those looking for campaign finance reform often cloak their discussions in terms of limiting the influence of large donors on the political process or in lessening the monetary burden of running for office. However, it is unusual when campaign reform truly benefits political challengers, and elected officials are loathe to vote for any reform that will tie their own hands regarding fundraising. As seen with BCRA, the legislation has not decreased the amount of money being funneled into political races. Instead, campaigns, parties, and independent groups are breaking fundraising records.

Elected officials don't like raising money, and they don't want to make it more difficult for themselves. While some view this fight primarily in terms of political parties, it is not really that simple. Campaign reform is about money and how that money can be raised and used, and that discussion is important to many sectors, including grassroots and independent organizations that are looking to influence elections. While political parties may want to remain the most powerful organizations at play in elections, their influence may be eroding because of social networking, issue-oriented organizations, and other new media.

It's simply impossible to get the influence of money out of politics, and all legislation has unintended consequences. It is said that, as BCRA was being debated in Congress, attorneys were already getting ready to establish 527s as an alternative for large donors. In essence, BCRA breathed new life into a loophole in the IRS legislation and made 527s a household term. While this does not bode well for future campaign finance reform, it does provide a more realistic look at potential outcomes. Simply put, you cannot change one thing without causing changes in others. Those involved in campaign reform are often willing to take this risk because of the potential to limit the influence of big donors in elections. It is a complicated process, and it is an ugly process, and the results are often mixed. But, in the end, it is reflective of the American system of government, which is based on compromise and the allocation of resources. Thus, the political shell game continues.

## NOTES

1. Coleman McCarthy, "A Man of Thought and Action," *Washington Post*, 13 Dec. 2003.
2. Neil Tickner, "Candidate Funding a Top Priority for New Members of Congress," University of Maryland 2000, www.newsdesk.umd.edu/archive/release.cfm?year=2000&ArticleID=266 (16 Aug. 2009).
3. John Franzen, "Consultants and clients," in D. D. Perlmutter (ed.), *The Manship School Guide to Political Communication* (Baton Rouge: Louisiana State University Press, 1999), 295–302.
4. Franzen, 'Consultants and Clients,' 300.
5. Larry Powell and Joe Cowart, *Political Campaign Communication: Inside and Out*, (Boston: Allyn & Bacon, 2003), 217.
6. Powell and Cowart, *Political Campaign*, 216.
7. Jennifer Steen, "Maybe You Can Buy an Election, but Not With Your Own Money," *Washington Post*, 25 June 2000, B1.
8. Jill Lawrence, "Bush Breaks Fund-Raising Record," *USA Today*, 1 July 1999, 10A.
9. Powell and Cowart, *Political Campaign*, 216.
10. John Rowley, e-mail message to author, 1 Dec. 2009.
11. Rowley, e-mail message to author, 1 Dec. 2009.
12. Fair Elections Now Act Bill Summary, Fair Elections Now, www.fairelectionsnow.org/more/summary (5 Oct. 2009).
13. Arthur Delaney, "Rep. John Larson: Political Fundraising Now 'Borders on Insanity,'" 15 Oct. 2009, www.huffingtonpost.com/2009/10/15/rep-john-larson-political_n_321525.html (12 Nov. 2009).
14. Fair Elections Now Act Bill Summary, Fair Elections Now.
15. Megan Moore, "The Four Tops Party On," 21 Oct. 2009, www.followthemoney.org/press/ReportView.phtml?r=402 (26 Nov. 2009).
16. Joe Cowart, e-mail message to author, 9 Dec. 2009.
17. Rowley, e-mail message to author, 1 Dec. 2009.
18. Rowley, e-mail message to author, 1 Dec. 2009.

19. Federal Register, "FEC Rules and Regulations, Internet Communications," 12 April 2006, www.fec.gov/law/cfr/ej_compilation/2006/notice_2006-8.pdf (15 Dec. 2009).

20. Cyrus Khron, "Slate Alum Cyrus Krohn, now Online Guru for the Rnc, is Injecting Consumer Savvy into E-Campaigning," *Politics*, Nov. 2008, 22–23.

21. Pew Research Center Publications, "Internet Overtakes Newspapers as Research Outlet," 23 Dec. 2008, pewresearch.org/pubs/1066/internet-overtakes-newspapers-as-news-source (9 June 2009).

22. Rowley, e-mail message to author, 1 Dec. 2009.

23. Rowley, e-mail message to author, 1 Dec. 2009.

24. Brody Mullins & Ianthe Jeanne Dugan, "Mega-Bundlers up Financing Ante," *Wall Street Journal*, 5 Nov. 2008, online.wsj.com/article/SB122584462604899359.html (12 Dec. 2009).

25. Mullins and Dugan, "Mega-Bundlers."

26. Supreme Court of the United States, Federal Election Commission v. Wisconsin Right to Life, www.supremecourtus.gov/opinions/06pdf/06-969.pdf (14 Nov. 2009).

27. Memorandum Opinion, "Christopher Shays & Martin Meehan, Plaintiffs, v. Federal Election Commission, Defendant," 18 Sept. 2004, www.fec.gov/pages/bcra/shays_meehan_mem_opinion_dc.pdf (15 Nov. 2009).

28. David Silverman, "Supreme Court Allows Corporate-Sponsored Issue Ads to Mention Candidates—Watch For Even More Political Advertising Next Year," 28 June 2007, www.broadcastlawblog.com/tags/bcra/ (17 Dec. 2009).

29. U.S. Court of Appeals, "Christopher Shays, Appellee, Cross-Appellant, v. Federal Election Commission, Appellant, Cross-Appellee," www.campaignlegalcenter.org/attachments/1874.pdf (17 Dec. 2009).

30. *Citizens United v. FEC*, "Case Summary," www.fec.gov/law/litigation/citizensunited.shtml (16 Dec. 2009).

31. Jeremy Jacobs, "The Case That Could Change the Race," *Politics*, Oct. 2009, 39.

32. Jacobs, "The Case," 40.

33. Library of Congress, "Citizens United v. FEC and the Future of Campaign Finance Reform," www.loc.gov/law/help/citizens-united.php (16 Dec. 2009).

34. Adam Liptak, "Justices Are Pressed for Broad Ruling in Campaign Case," *New York Times*, 9 Sept. 2009, www.nytimes.com/2009/09/10/us/politics/10scotus.html (16 Dec. 2009).

35. Jacobs, "The Case," 41.

36. Adam Liptak, "Justices, 5-4, Reject Corporate Spending Limit," *New York Times*, 21 Jan. 2010, A1.

37. Raymond LaRaja, *Small Change: Money, Political Parties, and Campaign Finance Reform*, (Ann Arbor: University of Michigan Press, 2008).

## BIBLIOGRAPHY (PARTIAL LIST)

Fair Elections Now Act Bill Summary, Fair Elections Now, www.fairelectionsnow.org/more/summary (5 Oct. 2009).

Franzen, John. "Consultants and Clients." In D. D. Perlmutter (ed.), *The Manship School Guide to Political Communication* (Baton Rouge: Louisiana State University Press, 1999), 295–302.

Jacobs, Jeremy. "The Case That Could Change the Race." *Politics*, Oct. 2009, 39.

LaRaja, Raymond. *Small Change: Money, Political Parties, and Campaign Finance Reform* (Ann Arbor: University of Michigan Press, 2008).

Liptak, Adam. "Justices Are Pressed for Broad Ruling in Campaign Case." *New York Times*, 9 Sept. 2009, www.nytimes.com/2009/09/10/us/politics/10scotus.html (16 Dec. 2009).

Liptak, Adam. "Justices, 5-4, Reject Corporate Spending Limit." *New York Times*, 21 Jan. 2010, A1.

Powell, Larry & Joe Cowart. *Political Campaign Communication: Inside and Out* (Boston: Allyn and Bacon, 2003).

Silverman, David. "Supreme Court Allows Corporate-Sponsored Issue Ads to Mention Candidates—Watch For Even More Political Advertising Next Year," 26 June 2007, www.broadcastlawblog.com/tags/bcra/ (17 Dec. 2009).

Supreme Court of the United States, *Federal Election Commission v. Wisconsin Right to Life*, www.supremecourtus.gov/opinions/06pdf/06-969.pdf (14 Nov. 2009).

# Afterword

## Corporations Are Given a Free Rein

As this book was in the final stages of completion, the United States Supreme Court issued a ruling on campaign finance laws that could lead to additional changes in the restrictions imposed on campaigns and corporations that participate in the campaign process—particularly in terms of third-party participants such as the 527 groups. The decision also re-ignited the old debate: Freedom of Speech versus the Ability of the Rich to Buy elections. And, of course, both sides immediately started working on ideas for either (a) getting a different ruling or a different law, or (b) taking advantages of the new leniencies suggested by the ruling.

The ruling concerned a suit filed by Citizens United against the Federal Election Commission. The issue involved a documentary (*Hillary: The Movie*) released during the Democratic primaries of 2008 that was largely an attack on Hillary Clinton's 2008 presidential candidacy. New York Times reporter Adam Liptak described the work as "a 90-minute stew of caustic political commentary and advocacy journalism."[1]

Lower courts had ruled that the movie was a work of advocacy journalism and thus in violation of that part of the Bipartisan Campaign Reform Act of 2002 which banned the broadcast or mass transmission of "electioneering communications" paid for by corporations or labor unions within 30 days before primaries and 60 days prior to a general election. As a result, the film was shown in only six cities, but was available on DVD or via the Internet.

The legal issue facing the court was a relatively narrow legal issue in terms of how to apply Campaign Finance Laws campaign finance laws to movies. If the law banned such a documentary, did it also mean that a classic movie such as *Mr. Smith Goes to Washington* could not be aired during the specified time frames prior to an election?

Political observers had been waiting on the decision, but expected it to apply to that narrow issue. Instead, the Supreme Court considered the case in terms of the broader issue of corporate influence on elections. The resulting 5-to-4 ruling broke on ideological lines, with the five conservative judges in the majority and the four liberal judges in the minority.[2]

The result, though, was a ruling that *USA Today* described as one that would lead to "a new era for campaign spending."[3] *The New York Times* wrote that the decision "handed lobbyists a new weapon" that would "increase the power of organized interest groups at the expense of candidates and political parties."[4] In a rare instance in which a sitting president criticized a Supreme Court decision, President Obama joined the chorus of critics, calling the decision "a major victory for big oil, Wall Street banks, health insurance companies and the other powerful interests that marshal their power every day in Washington to drown out the voices of everyday Americans."[5] He continued his attack in this weekly radio address the following week. "This ruling opens the floodgates for an unlimited amount of special interest money into our democracy," he said. "It gives the special interest lobbyists new leverage to spend millions on advertising to persuade elected officials to vote their way—or to punish those who don't."[6]

Opponents of the ruling immediately attacked the legality of the decision. They noted that, in terms of legal theory, the ruling overturned two Supreme Court precedents—a move that is counter the court's standard of following previous court precedents in making a ruling. The first previous ruling was *Austin v. Michigan Chamber of Commerce*, a 1990 decision that upheld restrictions on corporate spending in campaigns. The second was *McConnell v. Federal Election Commission*, a 2003 decision that upheld legality of that portion of the Bipartisan Campaign Reform Act that restricted campaign spending by corporations and unions.

## OPPOSITION CONCERNS

The potential for corporations to dominate elections was the major concern of those who opposed the ruling. As Zeleny concluded, the "ruling upends the nation's campaign finance laws, allowing corporations and labor unions to spend freely on behalf of political candidates."[7] *USA Today* agreed, writing in an editorial, "Think American elections are already grossly distorted by special interests? . . . It's about to get a lot worse."[8]

Democrats, in particular, were upset. Mitch Stewart, Director of Organizing for America (on behalf of President Obama), sent out an e-mail that said, "With no limits on their spending, big oil, Wall Street banks, and health insurance companies will try to drown out the voices of everyday Americans—and Republicans seem ecstatic."[9] The extreme version of this argument was expressed by Democratic Senator Alan Grayson of Florida who argued, "The Supreme Court in essence has ruled that corporations can buy elections. If that happens, democracy in America is over. We cannot put the law up for sale and award government to the highest bidder."[10]

Indeed, that scenario seemed likely. Immediately following the ruling, several groups that were active in the 2008 election reported that they would spend more money in 2010 and 2012.[11] Such an increase in spending would lean more favorably for Republicans than Democrats. While the ruling hypothetically applied to both corporations and unions, the group with the most upward potential was the corporate side—groups that sided more with Republicans. That means Republicans are likely to see a major infusion of cash from businesses over the next few years. Most of the support is likely to come in the form of independent expenditures, rather than donations directly to campaigns. As Democratic Senator Russ Feingold wrote following the decision, "I fear that our elections will become like NASCAR races—underwritten by companies."[12]

Beyond the financial implications for campaigns, the ruling created at least three other concerns. First, it is likely to be more beneficial to incumbents than to challengers and thus create an unfair advantage for the incumbent. Incumbents are in the strongest position to develop ties with corporations and are already in office and dealing with legislation that affects those corporations.

Second, there is a potential intimidation factor involved. Should an office holder be reluctant to support legislation beneficial to a particular corporation? As *USA Today* noted in its editorial on the topic, "All it will take is an implicit threat to a member of Congress, from say, a large bank that despises the idea of having to answer to a consumer financial regulatory commission: Vote for that and we'll spend $10 million against you this fall."[13]

Third, some opponents claimed that the decision also opens campaigns to donations from foreign companies.[14] Foreign donations were specifically banned under the McCain-Feingold BCRA. The court's decision made no distinction between American and foreign companies, potentially opening the door for donations from Asia and Europe. As one critic noted, "the ruling puts a big 'open for business' sign on the US election system inviting virtually any foreign national, foreign corporation or even foreign government spend to their hearts content on their candidate of choice."[15]

## ARGUMENTS IN SUPPORT OF THE DECISION

The main argument in support of the decision is the traditional "Freedom of Speech" issue. The argument: Freedom of Speech that applies to individuals should also apply to businesses. That theme was consistent throughout the decision.

Supporters of the decision also discounted the opponents concerns about "buying elections," noting that several states already had similar laws and had not been faced with excessive donations.[16] Indeed, the Democratic critics probably overplayed their criticism on this point. Feingold, for example, noted that the 2008 presidential election cost $2 billion for the candidates and their supporters, but that sum was minor compared to the $743 billion in profits that Fortune 500 companies made that year.[17] The catch, of course, is that those companies would face a shareholder revolt if they spent much of their profits on campaigns. Still, a one-percent investment from such companies would total more than $7 million—more than three times the amount spent by all of the players in 2008.

Second, while observers constantly complain about the negative impact of money on political campaigns, the process does not always work that way.[18] In fact, there is little evidence that the candidate with the most money wins the election. Generally, campaigns must have enough financial funds to be competitive; but, once that level of competitiveness is reached, additional funds seem to have little or no additional impact. If both candidates have enough money to communicate with the voters, the voters seem capable of reducing the impact of any financial advantage that any candidate might have.

Third, there seems to be little, if any, link between corporate contributions and electoral impact.[19] Past research indicates that many corporations donated to political activities out of a sense of obligation and that a reduction or elimination of such participation did not result in any loss of influence on their part. However, in the past, such participation was minimal. Whether the potential for unlimited participation will increase influence remains to be seen.

Fourth, other nations with minimal regulations have not faced major problems. In Australia, for example, both individuals and corporations can make unlimited donations to candidates. Further, the nation also has few disclosure laws. Still, political corruption has not been a major factor there.[20]

## CONCLUSION

The 2010 Supreme Court ruling will take time for all of the participants to figure out. Still, the new court decision offers new opportunities for those who play the political shell game. It opens up new avenues for funneling more money into campaign efforts, even if that money is still "hands off" for the campaigns themselves.

In the wake of the decision, Sen. Charles Schumer (D-NY) and Speaker of the House Nancy Pelosi said they would look for legislative ways to limit corporate spending.[21] However, Senator John McCain, whose signature legislation was the McCain-Feingold Act that became the BCRA, saw little future recourse for reformers. He noted the "sarcastic" and "skeptical" comments of the majority justices during the case, acknowledged the prospects for future reform were "dead," and added "I don't think there's much that can be done."[22]

Regardless, the decision may create a new series of ethical concerns for candidates. Bribery charges typically apply to office holders only when a specific donation—from a specific entity—can be tied to a specific vote or action by the office holder that benefits that entity. With the new infusion of cash coming to campaigns, office holders may find themselves under more scrutiny from the opposition. How many times did the individual vote for bills that benefited the corporation that spent millions of dollars on their behalf? And, of course, that candidate's opponent will frequently make the argument that the incumbent is "in the pocket" of a special interest group.

Sometimes the charge may be accurate. Other times, maybe not. Either way, the political shell game continues.

## NOTES

1. Adam Liptak, "Justices, 5-4, Reject Corporate Spending Limits," *New York Times* (January 22, 2010): A1.
2. *Citizens United v. Federal Election Commission,* Appeal to the U.S. Supreme Court from the U.S. District Court for D.C., No. 08-205. Decided January 21, 2010.
3. Fredeka Schouten and Joan Biskuic, "It's a New Era for Campaign Spending," *USA Today* (January 22, 2010): 1A.
4. David D. Kirkpatrick, "Lobbyists Get Potent Weapon in Campaign Ruling," *New York Times* (January 22, 2010): A1, A16.
5. Quoted by Liptak, "Justices, 5-4, Reject Corporate Sending Limits," p. A1.
6. Darlene Superville, "President Blasts Supreme Court over Citizens United Decision," *Huffington Post* (January 27, 2010).
7. Jeff Zeleny, "Political Fallout from the Supreme Court Ruling," *New York Times* (January 21, 2010).
8. "Court's Campaign Ruling Threatens the Public Interest," *USA Today* (January 22, 1010): 8A.
9. Mitch Stewart, "A Stampede," *Organizing for America* e-mail: (January 22, 2010).
10. Quoted by Kirkpatrick, "Lobbyists Get Potent Weapon," p. A16.
11. Brody Mullins, "Big Donors Plan Boost in Campaign Spending," *Wall Street Journal* (January 22, 1010): A6.
12. Russ Feingold, "High Court Opens the Floodgates," *USA Today* (January 22, 2010): 9A.

13. "Courts Campaign Ruling," p. 8A.

14. Zachary Roth, "Reformers: Court Decision Creates 'Huge Opening' for Foreign Companies to Sway Elections," *TPM Muckraker* (January 24, 2010), http://tpm-muckraker.talkingpointsmemo.com/2010/01/.

15. Josh Marshall, "Bring on the Foreign Money," *Talking Points Memo,* (January 25, 2010), http://www.talkingpointsmemo.com.

16. Bradley A. Smith, "'Pure Science Fiction,'" *USA Today* (January 22, 2010): 8A.

17. Feingold, "High Court Opens the Floodgates."

18. David D. Kirkpatrick, "A Buck for Your Vote, Sir? (Prove It)," *New York Times* (January 24, 2010): WK1, WK3.

19. Kirkpatrick, "A Buck for Your Vote."

20. Kirkpatrick, "A Buck for Your Vote."

21. Alexander Bolton and Aaron Blake, "Dems Plan to Push Bill to Limit Impact of Campaign Ruling," *The Hill,* http://thehill.com/homenews/campaign/77261-supreme-court-strikes-down-campaign-finance-restrictions.

22. "McCain: Campaign Finance Report Is 'Dead," *Face the Nation* (January 24, 2010), www.cbsnews.com/stories/2010/01/24/ftn/main6136386.shtml.

# Index

# About the Authors

**Melissa M. Smith** is an assistant professor of communication at Mississippi State University. Her research specializes in political communication with an emphasis on technology and campaigns. She also researches in the area of religion and politics. Her work has been published in *Communication Research Reports*, the *Journal of Media and Religion*, and *Politics* magazine. She has several years' experience as a newspaper reporter and television news producer that complement her teaching and scholarship. She earned her Ph.D. from the University of Alabama.

**Glenda C. Williams** is an associate professor of telecommunication and film at the University of Alabama. Her research specializes in political communication with an emphasis on broadcasting and campaigns. She also researches in the area of media marketing and promotion. Her work has been published in journals such as *Communication Research Reports*, *Communication Law & Policy*, and *The Journal of Promotion Management*. She worked in cable marketing for several years, and has more than 20 years experience as a political campaign consultant, specializing in radio ads. She earned her Ph.D. from the University of Alabama.

**Larry Powell** (Ph.D., University of Florida) is a professor of communication studies at the University of Alabama at Birmingham. He is also the author or coauthor of a number of other books, including *Political Campaign Communication: Inside and Out* (with Joseph Cowart), *Interviewing: Situations and Contexts* (with Jonathan Amsbary), and *Surviving Group Meetings* (with Amsbary, et al). He has served as a political consultant for campaigns in 26 states.

**Gary A. Copeland** (BA, MA California State University, Fresno; Ph.D., The Pennsylvania State University) is professor and chair of telecommunication and film and professor of communication studies at the University of Alabama. He has also taught at the Universitat Klagenfurt in Klagenfurt, Austria and the University of Aruba. Dr. Copeland is primarily known for his research in political advertising though he has written in several areas of study. He is coauthor of four books: *Broadcasting/Cable and Beyond*, 3rd ed., a telecommunication text; *Negative Political Advertising: Coming of Age*, a research text on negative political advertising; *Manipulation of the American Voter: Modern Political Commercials*, a research text that describes the effects and effectiveness of political advertising; and *Inside Political Campaigns: Theory and Practice* which reveals the art and science of political campaign consulting. He is coeditor of *Critical Questions: Invention, Creativity, and the Criticism of Discourse and Media*, a critique of critical discourse. His work has appeared in such publications as *The Harvard International Journal of Press/ Politics*, *Critical Studies in Mass Communication*, *Journalism Quarterly*, and *Journal of Broadcasting and Electronic Media*. He also has practical as well as academic experience as he has served as a paid political consultant to local, state, and federal campaigns and has consulted internationally.

**Barry P. Smith** is an assistant professor of communication at Mississippi University for Women. His primary areas of research include political communication (with an emphasis on technology) and video games (with an emphasis on entertainment as a media effect). His work has been published in *Communication Research Reports* and *Playing Video Games: Motives, Responses, and Consequences*. His professional experience includes television production and graphic design. He earned his Ph.D. from the University of Alabama.

**Lauren Reichart Smith** obtained her Ph.D. from the University of Alabama and began as an assistant professor of public relations at Auburn University in 2010. Her primary research interests lie in media portrayals and effects, with a special emphasis on media portrayal research within the realm of social networking and social media. She has presented her work at ICA, AEJMC, and BEA.

www.ingramcontent.com/pod-product-compliance
Ingram Content Group UK Ltd.
Pitfield, Milton Keynes, MK11 3LW, UK
UKHW012042150926
475560UK00001B/137